A Soulmates Twin Flame

A Soulmates

Twin Flame

It's not just another love story

Sarah J Provost

Memoir

Copyright © 2018 Sarah J Provost

All rights reserved. This book or any portion thereof may not be reproduced or used in any manner whatsoever without the express written permission of the publisher except for the use of brief quotations in a book review.

Printed in the United States of America

First Printing, 2018

ISBN 9780692130582

Independently Published

Cover photos by Gerard Provost

Cover design by Sarah Provost

Table of Contents

About Us 1

How we met 3

The Start of Wonderful 6

The Adventure Begins 15

As the Love Blossoms 31

The Next Doorway 37

Life, It Happens 56

Time for Something New 66

Ready or Not 74

Big Changes and Fun 89

Jerry's Canvas 101

Family Time 111

A Whole Lotta Love 123

New Experiences 128

Painting the Walls 134

Murphy Spends the Weekend 140

Roll with It 145

Sex and Drugs 154

The Things We Learn 165

Creative Sexy Romance 174

Excitement Awaits 181

An Amazing Husband 185

Just the Two of Us 193

Fury and Fun 199

When a House is a Home...209

The Fairytale...213

The Unknown...234

Together with Family..239

All the Days of my Life 245

This is dedicated to my husband,

my love, my twin flame.

Jerry, I love you!

About Us
The Yin and the Yang

Let me tell you a little about who I used to be. I was born under the sign of Taurus to an average family with a house and a yard and a dog in an average town in Massachusetts. Sarah (that's me,) the teenage version, had long, dark hair and was even considered beautiful by some. It sounds boastful, I know, but I did enjoy attracting the boys when I wasn't hiding behind my hair. It was like a super power among my more average qualities. I was compassionate and affectionate (bordering on neurotic); curious (well, okay, nosey); shy, yet spontaneous; I was a private person except when I wasn't; I struggled to communicate and hid my feelings unless I was screaming from the rafters about some wild adventure I was on; I had so much love to give, but jealousy sometimes got in the way. I was an average girl, of humble beginnings, but I was determined to live an above-average life. To prove the point, I skipped college and moved in with my boyfriend, ready for freedom, fun, and life. In less than a month, he hit the road, and I was left with bills, rent and a job as a waitress.

Enter Jerry (his legal name is Gerard, but he doesn't answer to that), an impatient, big-mouthed, overgrown hippie with a short fuse. I also saw his good traits: he was creative, smart, and adventuresome—the outrageous yin to my timid yang. Mostly, he'd been raised by a single mom, but there were a few years at the hands of an abusive stepfather. He was 25 to my 19, a *real* man who had served in the army and studied culinary arts. He was a worldly sort of guy, and I couldn't help but be impressed with how much life he had lived in a quarter century.

Jerry would say anything to get a laugh, and I do mean anything. But he was kind, right from the start, if not a touch outrageous. In those early days, I saw him stretch to the top shelf and pull a can down for an old lady at the grocery store. "It sucks to be tall," he said to her and flashed his toothy Jerry grin as he put the can of niblet corn in her cart. The old woman smiled up at him, charmed and taken aback in the same breath. I knew exactly how she felt.

How we met

Love is carefree

  I walked into work one afternoon in the summer of 1996, stopping to fix my hair in the dishwashing area. A new chef, Jerry, had started, and I wanted to check him out. I got a glimpse and kept walking. A few weeks later, he invited me out for drinks.

  "It's a regular thing," he said. "Me and the bartenders and the servers. Want to join us?"

  "Sounds fun," I said. "But I'm not old enough. I'm what you call 'under the legal limit.'" I felt like a kid admitting that to him. I was scared of getting caught and thought about what I would do if someone asked for an ID. Jerry was not someone I was interested in, and I was with these people every day. What is so fun about sitting at a bar talking? That thought went through my head along with a little voice that kept saying, boring, *boring!*

  "Oh, jailbait!" He laughed. "Don't worry about that. You're going with me, and I know everybody there. You won't have any problems." Jerry was a little full of himself, but this wasn't a date, just a night out with the crew. What did I have to lose?

  Drinking after work, which to my surprise was fun, became a habit soon enough, and blowing my tip money on drinks left me short on rent. Living independently wasn't all it was cracked up to be. I would have to find a cheaper way to let the good times roll or discover a way to make ends meet. I put out the word among the servers that I could use a roommate to share expenses. A few nights later, Jerry cornered me at the bar.

"What's this I hear about you looking for a roommate?" he asked. For the first time since we'd met, he had a serious look on his face.

"I have lived alone for many months now, and it's a little more than I can handle financially," I admitted. "I need a roommate to split the bills."

"Well, lucky me! I have been looking for an apartment to get out of my mom's house, but so far I have found nothing," he said.

"You live with your mom at age 25?" I asked. I tried not to look shocked.

"Yes, I came back a few months ago to help her. I had a great job in Texas and planned on going back, but shit happens, and I landed this job. So, I'm here for a while. Your apartment could be the perfect solution. For both of us." He flashed his trademark Jerry grin.

Jerry and I spent many nights going out or talking on the phone, sharing stories and getting to know each other a little more. I learned some of the crazy shit he did involving spontaneity and binge drinking. He told me how he was a deadhead and followed the Grateful Dead tour bus for nine months. Jerry also told me a little about an abusive stepfather and what he experienced with him. He heard all about the crazy shit I did, from my nightly adventures and sneaking out of the house to moving around a little. I told him about my parents getting divorced, but still putting us kids first and showing us plenty of love. Their divorce gave me an opportunity to move to the city for a year and have a blast before going back to the country. I might have been young, but I was a girl on a mission of fun and adventure. Jerry didn't think I was foolish. Despite the age difference, we shared similar qualities, but I didn't have an interest in dating him. Jerry was just a fun distraction.

When he moved in, we took our mutual immaturity to a whole new level. One night Jerry washed his hands and splashed me. *Ok, two can play at this game.* I grabbed a cup of water and threw it at him. I knew the game wasn't over and started running. He threw an even bigger cup of water at me. I grabbed two full spray bottles of water and chased him down like a bad, bad doggie. Every time he stopped to fill his cup, I soaked him, from head to toe. I won that game, hands down! I couldn't remember when I had laughed so hard, and Jerry—wet clothes clinging to him—looked like a young boy on summer vacation who had been playing with the water hose.

"Just so you know, I am not looking for a serious relationship. I still want to move back to Texas at some point. I am focused on my career and having fun," Jerry said one night. I started to say that playing with water bottles wasn't my idea of foreplay, but I didn't

"I am not looking for serious either. I just need a roommate to help. It's nice having a friend and someone to talk to at home," I responded.

After a night of fun and laughter getting to know each other, we found a photo booth

The Start of Wonderful

Desires and Love

One evening, Jerry and I decided to stay home, rent a movie and save some money. We sat on the couch together with a few drinks and snacks.

As the movie played, we inched closer together until his hand was right next to mine, then right on top of my hand. Movie forgotten, and I stared into his beautiful eyes. At an unspoken cue, we leaned in a little closer to one another, and our lips met. He put his strong arms around me. A wonderful feeling went through me, head to toe. It felt like a thousand butterflies in my stomach, and chills ran all the way to my toes. I was brimming with nervous energy and confusion, along with the thought, *I don't want this feeling to end*. I had other boyfriends, but this didn't feel the same, not by a country mile...

As days turned into weeks, we were roommates/friends who happened to sleep together, no big deal. Jerry's standard line was, "This isn't serious, I am focusing on my career." I kept my feelings close to my vest, but every time he said it I felt a little jab. Gone was the overgrown hippie who had moved in with me, replaced by a sexy, oddly charming man. Why would a guy this worldly look twice at a girl like me? I was drawn to him, nervous as a schoolgirl, but I tried to appear aloof. No big deal

At work, I would walk through the kitchen and notice Jerry watching me with a kindness in his eyes. He only talked about what was going on that evening, but the look in his eyes said the rest. The dialogue shifted from *Do you want to go out*? to *So . . . what are we doing tonight*? Fellow employees would ask if we were dating, and—after glancing at Jerry for a reaction—I'd say that we weren't.

On the nights when Jerry and I stayed home, we would hold hands on the couch, and the butterflies would flutter in my chest and my breath would quicken. Sometimes we'd kiss and lose track of the movie. Was this just a glorified friendship? Not for me, it wasn't. I hoped that Jerry would verbalize what I couldn't. We were going somewhere with this relationship, weren't we? Or was Jerry really going to leave and go back to Texas?

A month or so after he'd moved in, I invited my mom and her husband over for dinner. What's funny is that we didn't own a table, and neither of us remembered that tiny detail until they were already in the apartment. But Chef Jerry was also imaginative and the master of improvisation. He used an old toy trunk as a makeshift table for my parents, and I think they were charmed.

In December, Jerry and I bought a Christmas tree, lights, and decorations. This was far more than what roommates would do together, but neither of us admitted it yet. Christmas Eve, we got off work early and visited my mom and her husband along with my brother's family and my sister. On Christmas Day we celebrated and exchanged gifts at my dad's house, and then off to Jerry's mom's where we enjoyed a home cooked Christmas dinner.

"Well, that was a fun day," Jerry said sarcastically

"I know, right? Glad it's over," I replied

"You ready to go have a few drinks and get our game on?"

"Let's go. I have a feeling I might get lucky tonight."

We headed to our stomping grounds for the night and stayed until they booted us out around 2:00 am. We drank a lot that evening and played many games of pool, placing bets, mostly for sexual favors. It was always a competition between us. A few people came in that night and tried to win the table. Yeah right! That didn't happen. Jerry and I always knew how to step up our game and win.

When Christmas was over, we returned to our routines, ignoring the holiday glitter at home.

"Jerry, we have to take the tree and decorations down at some point," I said finally.

"Yeah, I know. I'm just not up for it. Where are we going to put everything?" he asked.

"I have an idea. Why don't we just take the tree and everything on it and put it in the dumpster? We can buy new shit next year."

"Sounds good to me, let's get it done."

We unplugged the tree, the lights and took down the few wall decorations, and together we carried everything out to the dumpster. It was a very fast Christmas cleanup at less than five minutes, and we had our living room back.

The next year, still with no commitment to one another, Jerry and I found a new place to live. It was old and rundown, but we had the whole third floor. To be honest, it was a dump. But what did that matter if we weren't going to be there much? We both worked a lot and, if not at work or out at a bar shooting pool, we drove around. Jerry and I would find new roads we had never been down just to see where they would take us. We liked getting lost, looking at the scenery and taking pictures.

"Sarah, look at that old house. I know about that house, I just never thought I would stumble across it," Jerry said on one of our drives.

"What do you know about it?" I asked

"They held witch trials there, back in the day. You see that old wooden stand, off in the distance? That's where the witch would be after she was found guilty."

"How do you know all this?"

"From the old ladies at the nursing home. Hey, could you please hand me the camera?"

Sarah J Provost

It was an odd way to connect with a man, but Jerry's aimless wandering was just like mine. My friends would look at me like I'd grown horns just because I wanted to follow a new road and find where it went. "Take me home now," more than one friend had insisted. I couldn't explain the attraction to exploring a new path, to seeing where the next bend in the road would lead. Maybe I'd spot a waterfall or a bird of prey. Maybe I'd run into a dead-end or straight off of an unforeseen cliff. Not knowing what lay ahead was the beauty of it all, and Jerry got that. My friends may have called it careless behavior, but with Jerry, it felt carefree. We lived in the moment without regrets.

One night after wandering the backroads, we came home and made love, maybe for the first time. I mean, the sex was good, but this time I was on an emotional high, and Jerry clung to me with a fierce intensity. "I'm falling in love with you," Jerry said. He looked vulnerable, naked down to his soul. I put coy aside and admitted what I had been feeling. *I love you too* didn't begin to sum it up. Jerry was like that winding road with hidden surprises. I couldn't wait to see what lay ahead.

We continued to work together but didn't deny to anyone that we were a couple. We had one rule that we both agreed on. Once we walked through the doors at the restaurant, it was not Jerry and Sarah the couple, but the chef and a server.

Another month went by and it was time to move again. We had gotten so fed up living in a dump. The new apartment we found was beautiful, and just remodeled. There was also a washer and dryer. I was excited about that, no more going to laundromats. There was a week wait to move in, so we had asked my dad if we could stay with him for a week.

"Smile"

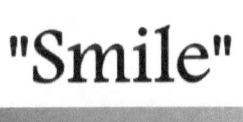
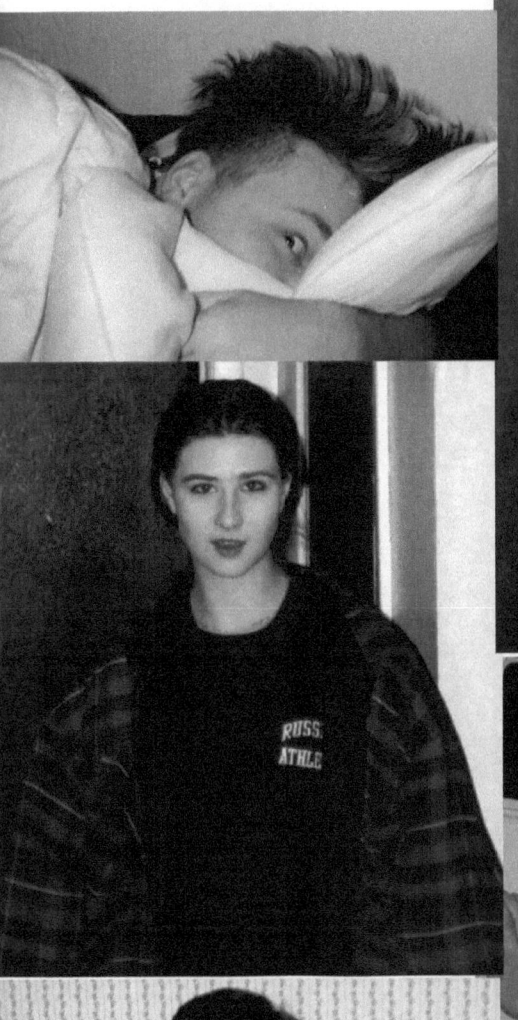

Random Surprise Photos

Our Early Days

Smile or Don't

The Adventure Begins

Music and Magic Mushrooms

Our new apartment was finally ready. We were eager to move in. There was one problem with this apartment, no thermostat for heat. The house was hot, and we couldn't figure out how to lower the heat, so we opened a window. Two minutes later, the phone rang. It was the landlord asking if everything was ok because we opened a window. He explained that he controlled our heat. After a few more phone calls, we figured out what windows we could and could not open.

It had been a long cold winter thus far that year, and I complained to Jerry about it one morning.

"I am so tired of the cold, I can barely breathe when we go outside," I said.

"Yeah, I know, me too," he replied.

"I would love to spend just one week away from all this cold. Have you ever been to Florida? I mean, work's slow, so we could probably get the time off."

"Sounds like fun, but can we afford it?" Jerry asked.

"Well, Mom and her husband are vacationing in Daytona Beach. What if we just show up there?" I suggested.

Within two days we were making our way down the coast to Florida. We decided to call in sick to work the day we left and said there was an emergency and we would be back in about a week.

We arrived in Virginia late that first night, got a room and I told Jerry to look for hidden cameras as I thought we were part of a new horror movie being made. We were way off the beaten path, and I was terrified. Jerry admitted that it didn't seem like the safest place he'd stayed, but it was only for one night.

"You're not leaving my side," I said to him. "If I need a smoke, so do you. If I wake up, then you're getting up too, and don't even think about leaving me in that room alone, are we understood?" Once the sun came up, we hit the road again.

As we entered Orlando, Florida, I spotted a Skycoaster, a tall thrill ride. A big sign read *Experience the closest thing to jumping out of a plane besides jumping out of a plane!*

"We have to try it," I said to Jerry.

Within ten minutes we were bound together and strapped into harnesses. The ripcord was on Jerry's side. I knew I'd be too scared to pull it. As they raised us in the air, I was scared and excited simultaneously. We held onto each other tight with our arms intertwined. As we reached the top he said, "Are you ready? I am going to pull it." We were soaring like birds in the sky while never letting go of each other. When we finally planted our feet back on the ground, we continued holding one another, laughing out loud.

"Wow, what a rush!" I said.

"That was fucking awesome," he replied.

Our Skycoaster Adventure

Sarah J Provost

After our little adventure, we found a place to stay that night and were off to Disney World the next morning. Jerry and I both wanted to let the kid inside us out and feel a rush. We went to MGM studios which had the most thrill rides. Our favorite ride there was the Tower of Terror. It's a freefall thrill ride in an elevator based on the Twilight Zone. We rode that multiple times that day. The next day we went to Magic Kingdom. That park was fun as well. It was geared towards the inner child in us. I had a blast walking around, having our pictures taken while we posed with Disney Characters, and I was overjoyed to see Cinderella's castle.

That evening we drove around looking at everything Florida had to offer. The next morning, we noticed how careless we had been when it came to money. We had enough to fill the tank and drive to Daytona Beach. I didn't know the name of my mom's hotel, but I knew it was on the main strip parallel to the ocean.

I said to Jerry, "I will know it when I see it and if not, we can pull into the fancy hotel parking lots and look for their car. I know they are here somewhere."

After searching a few hotel parking lots, we found their car. We parked, got out and Jerry let out a really horrible smelling fart. We walked into this beautiful hotel and found my folks having dinner. It was our lucky day, but my mom was in shock; she had no clue we were even thinking about taking a vacation.

We sat down with them, told a few little white lies and asked if we could spend a few days with them. After an hour we went back to the car to get our stuff. We looked at each other and broke out into laughter. The smell of Jerry's fart was still so powerful, and horrendous an hour later. Broke, conniving and smelly—that was us. But to me and Jerry, it was all part of the adventure.

We spent the next two days with my mom, enjoying her generosity at this luxury hotel. We frolicked in the pool, testing how long we could hold our

A Soulmates Twin Flame

breath underwater and who could sit on the bottom of the pool the longest. We were the only ones in the pool, so we ignored the no jumping rule and tried to see who could make a bigger splash doing cannonballs. We acted like teenagers, if that old. There were a lot of laughs that night. We explored Daytona Beach, bought a few souvenirs and partied over the next two days.

    Adventure week ended, and we knew we had to make our way back home. My mom gave us some cash, and we started our journey back. We took a different route home, hoping to see new things, or maybe it was to delay the inevitable. Home meant work and responsibilities and cold weather.

A Week of Spontaneous Fun

It was still winter in New England and I hated the cold. But Jerry and I found a way to play in the snow and stay warm at the same time. We would wait for big snow accumulations and listen to the radio for all the parking bans and store closings, then warm up the car and head out. We would find the roads with steep inclines that had a parking ban, so we didn't have to worry about hitting other cars, and we'd go car sledding. We also went to the empty parking lots and did *donuts*. After a few hours, we would go back home and relax. Something sent Jerry's imagination into overdrive.

"I have an idea, let's make our own hot tub," Jerry said.

I called around until I found a kiddie pool in the dead of winter, and we got to work. All four burners were going full blast on the stove, heating water to boiling while we partially filled the pool with the garden hose. When the pool was about halfway full, we shut the water off and dumped our pots of boiling water in. We ran back in the house, grabbed towels and got ready to get in. It was fifteen degrees out that evening, so we were quick to jump into our hot tub for warmth. Well, to our surprise, it was freezing. We jumped out of there so fast and booked it in the house laughing.

"Ok, I didn't expect to freeze my butt off after I got in the water," I said to him.

"No shit, that got cold fast." He was shivering as we cuddled together naked under a blanket.

"At least we tried, and it was fun," I said.

"Oh no, we're not done. I have another idea and we're going to try it," Jerry said.

"Alright, you know I'm willing to try anything. What's plan B?"

The next day Jerry bought a few things, so we could run the hose from inside the house with extremely hot water. We filled our pool again while adding pots of boiling water. We ran outside and got in. This time our hot tub was hot, but it didn't last long. We submerged ourselves in the warmth of the pool, but it was like somebody turned a switch, and suddenly we were cold again. But this time, we forgot towels. It was brutal running in the house naked and soaked. We jumped in the shower together to get warm and laughed while we held each other. We told a few friends about our hot tub adventure, and they looked at us like we were purple. They weren't far off: on hot tub day, we were, in fact, a mix of blue and purple.

Jerry and I continued to visit the bars and play pool when we couldn't figure out what else to do, but I quickly learned that Jerry couldn't handle hard liquor.

"When we go out, no more hard liquor. I have had enough with that shit," I said to him.

"What's your problem tonight?" he asked with a snotty attitude.

"There's no problem, but you get mean and rude for no reason on hard liquor. Stick with beer, and we will have no problems." He rolled his eyes at me.

"Who's gonna do all those crazy shots with you that you like?"

"I can do my shots while you drink your beer. I don't get mean like you do."

"Whatever," he said.

"Don't whatever me! Remember the last time we both had mixed drinks? All the guy did was ask me for directions, and you were ready to take his head off. I had to drag you out by the hand, and we had to leave before you started a fight- and don't forget the day before that, same stupid shit. I know you remember," I said to him.

Jerry followed my advice that night, and we had a good time. We left the bar that night when we were both ready, not me forcing him to leave.

A few months later we bought concert tickets to a *Phish* show in downtown Manhattan. We left the afternoon of the show and within a few hours, we were in the city, looking for the venue. Jerry was the driver and I oversaw navigation. I thought I was good at reading maps, but that was not the case. A GPS would have been awesome that day.

We drove around for a little over four hours trying to find this place. Jerry was getting so irritated with me. I would say take a left, and he would say "I can't, it's one-way." I did not realize what all the different icons on the map meant. A road atlas for New York was very different from the road atlases we used in the country. We were getting so irritated with each other, and at the same time laughing. Driving through Manhattan was different from anywhere else I had been. The traffic, people, one-way roads, shops, and skyscrapers—it was like nothing else I had ever seen.

When we finally found our destination, it was a bar, and the tickets we bought were for a Phish cover band. We were disappointed and left but chalked it off as a great Jerry & Sarah adventure.

Jerry and I went to many concerts —from some great 80's hairbands to reunion tours, and lots in between. I will tell you that my favorite concert was *Poison*. We saw them twice. We sang along at a Stevie Nicks show. Jerry also took me to my first *Grateful Dead* show (minus Jerry Garcia). That was a good time and a whole new crowd of people. Sometimes I couldn't help but laugh. I was a rock-n-roll girl, so this was different for me.

We never took the easy route though. Once Jerry wanted to show me a waterfall in Sanderson Falls in Massachusetts. There was a trail you follow to get to the waterfall, but he knew a better way, of course. The hike itself was fun as it was not a mapped-out trail, and a few areas were tricky to navigate. When we got to the waterfall it was beautiful. It was also romantic to be in such a serene place with no one else there.

Over the next year, I realized that we shared a passion for adventure, spontaneity, thrills, and living life to its fullest. Anytime we had a chance to do something different or just get away, we did. We drove to Maine to play mini-golf, Boston to visit the Cheers Bar and walk along the cobblestone streets. We took a romantic getaway to the Poconos lovers' resort in Pennsylvania, and a road trip to New Jersey for thrill rides at Six Flags.

Jerry and I also spent many nights camping. One evening we went camping out in Huntington, Massachusetts, at a place called Indian Hollow. It was gorgeous, with beautiful open land for miles and a lake. Beyond its borders was woods all the way around the open field.

The large campground was by reservation only, and it was blocked off by security gates and fences with signs saying, "Do Not Enter" and "No Trespassing." Naturally, Jerry and I wanted to camp there. We parked the car as far off the road as we could and went around the locked gates, walked toward the water and set our tent near the lake.

Jerry and I collected firewood and got a fire going. I had a good time talking and drinking wine that evening around the open fire. There was not another soul for miles. All we heard was animals and the sounds of Mother Nature. We could be as loud as we wanted, and no one would hear us. It was early the next morning when we were awoken by a police officer telling us we were trespassing and needed to leave immediately. We gathered all our stuff together and left.

Jerry and I also liked to explore old abandoned places or buildings. One afternoon we went to an old amusement park. It was called Mountain Park and was shut down in the mid-80's. When we went, there were still many old games, food stands, and a couple of rides. They were all old, rusted and destroyed. You could see there had been multiple small fires over the years, as many games had fire damage and trash was everywhere. It was fun and creepy at the same time to walk around and sift through everything to see if maybe there were hidden mementos we could save. We found a few things, but nothing valuable.

Camping Adventures

Sarah J Provost

We celebrated my 21st birthday at home. Jerry and I bought liquor and had a few friends over. We spent the night drinking and talking. We celebrated Jerry's 27th birthday in a similar way-a party at home with food, friends, and fun.

One fun activity we did on Jerry's birthday was mushrooms. He had tripped on shrooms many times. I tried a couple of times with no luck. Every time I ate them, nothing happened. I tried again that night, and again nothing. Jerry and a few friends laughed and laughed, but I had no idea what was so funny. I was jealous and irritated.

I tried mushrooms one other time after that, except I made a concentrated tea with them. A friend and I drank the tea. Again, nothing for me, but my friend had a blast. Jerry could see I was disappointed.

"Sarah, I don't know what to tell you, you're different. I will say you are the first person I have met that couldn't trip off mushrooms," Jerry said to me.

"Well it's not fair, it looks like fun. I'm not wasting any more money on that shit," I said back to him.

"I'm not complaining. I like the fact that even when you drink like a fish, you're always fine. I don't understand how you've never gotten sick and have never had a hangover. Maybe you have a chemical imbalance or something," Jerry said with a smile.

Once we set out on an adventure, we didn't let anything get in our way. Our road trip to Six Flags in New Jersey proved that point. We headed out early in the morning. When we crossed the border into New Jersey, we stopped at a convenience store for a bite to eat. Jerry reached behind the driver's seat to grab the map and sliced his upper arm open, right on the bicep. I looked behind the seat, and there was a huge piece of glass sticking out.

I went into the store for first aid now instead of food. I came back out and Jerry was sitting in the passenger seat holding his arm up. When I was ready I asked him to lift his arm up, as he raised his arm and the muscle flexed, that slice ripped open even more with lots of blood. Jerry saw it, he became queasy and then passed out. I slapped him. He immediately woke up after that. I did my best to clean it and stop the bleeding. We figured we could go to first aid at the park.

We arrived, paid our admission and looked for first aid. We found the first aid and were told they couldn't do anything. He needed to go to the hospital to have it stitched up. We said no way! I again cleaned the wound, bandaged it, wrapped it. I said to Jerry, "Looks good baby, you'll be fine, let's go wait in line for the new roller coaster." We both kept extra bandages and gauze in our pockets just in case.

We went to wait in line for the new coaster called "The Medusa" We rode that ride multiple times. There were many roller coasters there, but our second favorite was a Batman coaster. Batman was more of a freefall roller coaster and it was a great thrill ride that had us both screaming. I had a blast that day, even having to take a few breaks to change bandages. Jerry declared the day "fucking awesome!" While driving home we passed by a hospital and didn't stop. Dr. Sarah was all he needed.

Jerry and I took many local day trips on our days off from work. We visited the bridge of flowers a couple of times in Shelburne Massachusetts, and a place called the "Potholes" also out in Shelburne. The potholes were fun and interesting. These potholes are a Mother Nature wonder and it's beautiful. Some say that these potholes were created from the last ice age. There are many pools of water and small waterfalls surrounded by huge glacier rocks you can climb and sunbathe on.

We spent many nights stargazing. We'd find the darkest areas we could, far away from light pollution. Sometimes we'd set up a telescope to look at the stars and always tried to watch the meteor showers. One night in particular, the darkness seemed to bring out the philosopher in Jerry.

"There is so much more out in the universe and beyond," he said. "If there wasn't, then it would just be an awful waste of space."

A few of our conversations would lead to talks about life on earth.

"What if life is just a big chess game? What if humans are all pawns?" He said.

"There could be a greater force at work that as humans we can't understand. Do we really have free will?"

Jerry was like a child whose curiosity could never be quenched. The more he knew, the more he wondered. If he wasn't taking a new journey down a forbidden highway, he was thinking about other universes.

"Think about it, Sarah. Do we really understand what fate is?"

I'd never met anyone quite like Jerry.

As the Love Blossoms

Love is forgiving

I walked in the door one afternoon after spending a few hours helping my sick dad and saw a bag packed near the door, I yelled out to Jerry.

"Jerry, I'm home," I said loudly.

"Get out!" he screamed from the bedroom.

"What did you just say to me?"

"You heard me, get out! You are the most selfish person I have ever met."

I left the house in tears and sat in the car for a while, then I drove around for about an hour and went back home. I walked into the bedroom where Jerry was lying down. I asked him what his problem was.

"You knew I needed my pills and said you would fill the prescription for me," he said.

"I did, I have them right here. I told you I was going to help my dad because he is sick and would be back in a few hours with your medication. I don't understand why you'd think I was being selfish. None of this was for me," I said to him.

"Can I have one now, please?" Jerry asked rudely.

"You still had a pill when I left, where is that one?"

"It's gone, and I need another. The pain is worse, just give me the pills."

"No, you obviously have a problem."

Jerry had lost his job as the executive chef because of a back injury he suffered while working and had to have surgery to repair a few ruptured discs.

He was given pain medication to help and the doctor had told us that his recovery would slow.

I walked out of the bedroom and went to sit on the couch. I was done talking to him, and I wasn't leaving my apartment. An hour later Jerry walked out and asked if he could sit next to me.

We sat on the couch together, and he apologized. He said that he never wanted to hurt me and had no idea why he packed a bag and said those words to me.

"Sarah, please forgive me. I am so sorry. The pain got the best of me, and I took it out on you. Again, I am so sorry, and I love you so much," he said to me with tears in his eyes.

"Jerry, I love you too and I want to help you. For us to get through this, I will keep these pills. You have become addicted. We should have not even needed a refill."

"Ok, just please tell me you can forgive me."

"I forgive you, but what you said was really hurtful. I love you, but don't give me an attitude if I tell you I'm not up for shooting the shit with you tonight."

I gave Jerry another pill that day and we watched a movie together. There was not much conversation between us.

"Sarah, could you please come into the bathroom for a minute?" Jerry asked early the next morning.

"Ok, I'm coming. Are you ok?"

"Yes, I am better than ok. Where are my pain meds?"

"I have them, and you're not getting one. Lets please see if we can go a few more hours."

"Can I have the bottle for a minute, please?"

"I'll show you the bottle and you can read the label if you want, but I'm not giving you any."

"Baby, c'mon, please just give me the bottle. I want to show you something."

"Fine, but I am not leaving this bathroom until I get that bottle back in my hands," I said very loud and clearly.

I gave Jerry the bottle of pills, and as he opened them, I was about to start yelling at him but was stopped dead in my tracks as I watched him dump all the pills in the toilet and flush them.

"Jerry, what are you doing? We might still need those," I asked in a panic.

"Sarah last night was a long night. As I lay there and watched you sleep for a while, my mind would not shut down. All I could see was the pain in your eyes, and that pain was caused by me. That hurt I saw in you was worse than my back pain. I don't want to act like that again, and I don't want you to worry that it could happen again, so this is for the best. I thought about just the back pain and realized that the pain wasn't bad enough to need medication. Sure, some moments were worse than others, but when we are happy and laughing, I don't even notice it," he explained to me.

"I'm not so sure. I can sense your pain when we do those exercises and I still think you might need something, but whatever, we'll try it your way. I'll come up with something to keep you laughing," I said back to him with doubt.

"I promise baby, we can do this. I just want to hear you laugh and see that smile again."

"Can we just get something to eat now? I'm hungry." I was done talking about the situation and didn't know what else to say. It was now a waiting game to see if Jerry could tolerate the back exercises we were told to do without meds.

That night we did our routine exercises, and I could hear a few painful groans, but when it was done, I reached out, hugged him, told him I loved him and said, "ok, let's get these clothes off so we can snuggle naked." Jerry never took another pill.

A few months had gone by since Jerry's back surgery, and I was not feeling good. I had started a new job as a server at another restaurant. We were both smokers, and out of the blue, cigarettes made me feel nauseous. I thought I was coming down with a cold or something. That nausea feeling got worse, and I couldn't smoke anymore.

I missed my next period and took a pregnancy test. The results came back positive. Jerry was excited; he said he was so in love with me and was ready to start a family. I was not so certain, not sure if I was ready to become a mom. I had so much fun over the last few years together that I didn't want to give it up. I was happy with just the two of us.

We talked about it for a while and agreed we were ready. We were still young, so we knew there would be time for just us again later in our lives.

"We will become mom and dad, have a family, raise wonderful kids, and then it will be back to the Jerry and Sarah show," he said.

Jerry started work at another restaurant as a chef. This restaurant was not as elegant as the place we met at, but he was in charge and they paid him well. We were also battling with the workman's comp issue.

Another month went by, and Jerry received a small settlement from workman's comp. We were paid up on the rent and he bought a bike and a new professional 35mm camera, that he showed me how to use. Jerry was into photography as a hobby when I met him, and I had learned to love it too. We took nature photos on our drives and old scenery photos. Both of us took random surprise photos of each other. I would grab a camera while he was taking a shower, pull the curtain open, and quickly snap a picture. Jerry would get so fed up with me.

I continued working as a server for a few more months, but the cigarette smoke was making sick, and not all establishments were 100% smoke-free yet. I couldn't take it any longer; I had to quit. I started a part-time job as a cashier down the road from where we lived.

Jerry and I had discussed baby names, both boy and girl names.

"Honey, we are having a girl, and her name is Isabelle!" Jerry said very loudly and abruptly one morning.

"Okay baby, whatever. The ultrasound is today, we'll find out soon enough," I said.

We went to the doctors that afternoon, and I watched Jerry jump up and down for joy like a child when we were told it was a girl.

"See, I told you we were having a girl. I dreamt about the baby being a girl. The name, well, I saw that on a street sign yesterday, but didn't get a chance to talk to you about it until this morning," Jerry said while still parading around the room waiting for the doctor to come back in.

March of 1999, and we were moving again. Jerry and I found a duplex for rent outside the city in a quiet neighborhood. We agreed that the place was perfect. The house had two floors with a yard on a dead-end street. Jerry was more than excited. He couldn't wait to buy a lawnmower as he had never lived in a house with a yard big enough to mow.

When I was seven months pregnant, we bought tickets to see a real Phish concert in Albany, New York. This time we made sure it was Phish and not a cover band. That was my first indoor show that was general admission. When we arrived, it was a large venue with long lines to enter. Inside, the place was packed to the hilt! General admission to an indoor concert, crazy! You could barely walk, there were so many people.

I had a good time in the beginning, and the music was great, but after almost two hours I was ready to leave. The smoke from all the marijuana became overwhelming and made me feel sick. Jerry loved it, he didn't need to bring his own, and there was plenty in the air to get you high. We had to leave; I felt awful.

That spring, we had a baby shower. That was a great day and Jerry catered the event. There were many women there, and a few men, all friends and family. As I was getting close to the last gift, Jerry came and sat next to me. I saved the biggest box for last. When I opened it, the box was full of paper. When I got through all the paper, there was a large baby bottle at the bottom.

Jerry opened the bottle and pulled out an engagement ring. He then got down on one knee.

"Sarah, will you marry me? I know what I said at the beginning of our relationship, but I never thought I would ever meet anyone like you."

"Yes, of course. You know how much I love you," I said. We both teared up a little

Jerry would tell me how beautiful I was every day, even though I thought I was as big as a house. (I had gained about 80 lbs. thus far and still gaining) We would lie in bed together, and he would keep his hands on my belly and wait to feel the baby kick or move. Jerry bought a device where you could listen to the heartbeat and sounds of the baby. He also sang and talked to her on many occasions. He loved to sing Led Zeppelin to her and couldn't wait to be a dad!

The Next Doorway

Life, Loss, and Unity

The day before my due date, Jerry took me on a boat road as he couldn't wait any longer. He was bouncing me up and down. I felt like I was on a rollercoaster ride. I don't know if he was intentionally trying to speed up my labor, but as I was getting ready for bed that night, my water broke.

I questioned if I was even in labor. We were at the hospital and I still didn't feel a cramp. A few hours after my water broke I began to feel it. That was a long night. The pain was intense, and my contractions were getting closer and worse as the hour's pass.

The doctor said I had to walk around to help my body. "Are you out of your mind," I asked him. Walking was impossible when a contraction came on. After many hours, they decided to give me a drug that would speed up the process, so I could at least get far enough along to have an epidural. A few more hours went by, and finally, I was given the good stuff. All the pain was gone from the waist down. Every five minutes Jerry would ask me how I was feeling or if I needed anything. He would ask the nurse if we were getting close to pushing time, and then I would hear him sigh when she said not yet. After watching him pace the room for hours, I was told that they were shutting off the pain meds because I needed to feel again to push. Jerry ran over to me.

"Baby, are you ready? The nurse said it's time," Jerry said as his smile went from ear to ear.

"No, I'm not ready, but do I have a choice? She's coming whether I'm ready or not," I said. I was now filled with fear and could feel the pain coming back. Even though Jerry and I went to Lamaze classes and I knew all about giving birth, I still couldn't understand how a watermelon was supposed to fit through something the size of a lemon. This was running through my head as the pain got worse, and nothing Jerry said helped subside that fear. I was told to push, and he was by my side for most of it, until he heard the baby's head was visible. Jerry ran to the edge of the bed and saw his daughter. He cried as he ran back to hold my hand. After fifteen hours of labor, our healthy baby girl was born on May 19th, 1999.

Over the next few months, Jerry and I loved being mom and dad to our sweet Isabelle. We spent many hours videotaping. I was usually the one behind the camera.

"Jerry, do that thing you do with her Tigger bear to make her laugh, please," I asked.

"She was just laughing. You didn't catch any of that on video?"

"I did, but only about a second. You were in the way and most of the video is you."

"What? I was not in the way. What are you talking about?"

"Okay, maybe you weren't quite in the way, but I think the video camera likes recording you."

"Give me the camera, please. I'll record for a few minutes."

I gave Jerry the video camera, while I played with Isabelle. He recorded a few times while the three of us played. Later that evening we watched the videos.

"Sarah, you got mostly me on video with a few seconds of Isabelle," he stated.

"Does it matter? We got a few seconds of her laughing. It was way more fun watching you on film. I like seeing videos of you and the silly shit you do," I responded.

"Let's check out the other videos," he said.

"Ha! See, you're no different. I am in every single shot and many of just me. Don't sit here and argue that I only tape you."

May 15th 1999

May 18th 1999

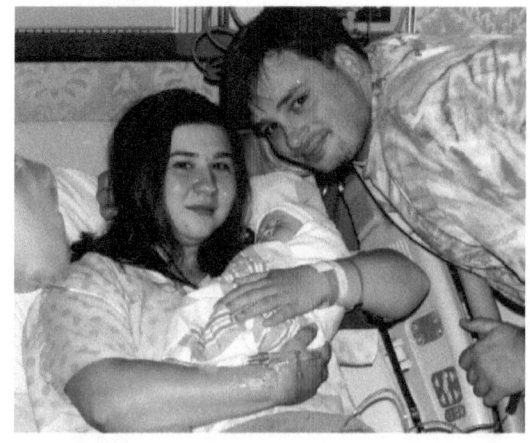

May 19th 1999

A Soulmates Twin Flame

Jerry was still working at the restaurant, and I stayed home with Isabelle. I had a bad feeling one afternoon and asked my mom to watch her while I went to see my dad. My father was very sick and had been in the hospital for a few months now. He had gotten married again four years earlier, and periodically I would see my stepmom there.

I just felt I needed to see my dad that day; it couldn't wait. I got to the hospital and went to his room. He had been asleep for about a week. He would wake up for a few minutes once or twice a day, but that was it.

"Hi, my Big Wid," he said. He'd called me that since I was a kid. I spent about twenty minutes there, told him I loved him and gave him a goodbye hug.

It was early the next morning when I got a phone call that my father had passed away during the night. I went back to the hospital to be with the family. I didn't stay long. He was on life support so the family could all say goodbye. It was hard to see him like that. I left before anyone decided it was time to pull the plug. I was so blessed to say goodbye to my dad while he was still here. I wanted the comfort of my family at home. Jerry was my rock for everything, and no matter what the day brought, seeing his face brought out my happiness.

My dad was 47 years old when he passed away on July 30th, 1999. I never imagined that such a good man could die so young. I found so much love with Jerry and Isabelle that it helped with the passing of my father. I believe that his passing was a blessing to the family as we all watched how sick he became over the last ten years. He was diagnosed with type 1 diabetes as a kid, and overtime it caused many other problems.

We were also in the planning stages for our wedding, which occupied my mind. We had set the date for March 25th, 2000. I told Jerry I would not settle for anything less than my dream wedding. Wow, there was a lot to do, from my dream dress with a long train; to the church; the florist; the cake; and the reception. It all seemed overwhelming while taking care of a newborn baby.

Sarah J Provost

My mom helped me find the dress. We had searched many bridal shops, but the dresses I liked were not the right size since I was still carrying all the extra pregnancy pounds. We finally found a dress that I loved that could be altered. I went for many fittings and had my dream dress, with a beautiful long train.

Jerry and I did the cake together, using a great local bakery that customized our order for the perfect (and perfectly delicious!) wedding cake.

Along with all the wedding planning, Jerry and I made sure we still had time for fun and us. That year we rang in Y2K with style and fun. We had his mom watch Isabelle overnight and we attended a New Years Eve party at a beautiful hotel that my mom had told us about. There was a huge ballroom where the party was. This was a new experience for us as it was formal. Jerry had to buy a few new things and I borrowed an outfit from a friend. The party was boring in the beginning, but as the drinks kicked in and the music became more upbeat, we had fun.

"Jerry, this is getting boring, and we are like the youngest couple here," I whispered to him while sitting at our table.

"I know, look at the couple over there. Hooray to them for still getting out at eighty years old," he replied.

"I'd say let's dance, but this is some pretty lame music."

"I see more frowns than I do smiles. Do you want another drink?"

"Sure, please. Oh my gosh, listen. You have to come do the electric slide with me," I insisted with a smile.

"Okay, fine, whatever, darling," Jerry said in a sarcastic tone.

"At least the music is getting better. I bet the final song of the night will be that song by *Prince* where he sings 'Gonna party like it's 1999'," I said jokingly.

A Soulmates Twin Flame

The evening did pick up, the food was good, and Jerry and I danced the night away. The song they played right before the clock struck midnight was the song by Prince that I mentioned to Jerry.

New Years Eve 1999

A Soulmates Twin Flame

My wedding day had arrived and very quickly, I might add. I felt anxious, nervous, and excited. I felt sleepy too, having gotten up at 5:00 am to have my hair and makeup done. After I got back, I got dressed, with a little help of course. I had a gold heart-shaped locket that my parents gave to me when I was young as my something old. For my something new my mother had given me a new heart-shaped locket to wear with the old one. I had something borrowed, and my garter was blue.

The photographer then came to start our pictures with my mom and sister. He took so many photos that morning. I had fun doing a photo shoot with the different props and all the traditional wedding photos of the bride. The photographer then went to the church to do a photo shoot with Jerry. There were many fun pictures that he did. We have a photo where Jerry is trying to run out of the church before I got there. Yeah, right! I knew he was just as excited as I was. Every time we talked about it over the last few weeks, he had a smile that went from ear to ear and always had to kiss me. I certainly wasn't complaining.

The limo had arrived to pick up me, my sister and my mom and bring us to the church. When I arrived, the photographer took a few more photos as I exited the limo and entered the church. The time had finally arrived, and I walked down the aisle toward the altar where Jerry was waiting for me. In place of my father, my brother gave me away on my special day. As I got close to Jerry, I could see tears of joy in his eyes. I was trying to make my brother walk a little faster as I just couldn't wait to get there. I felt like I had been waiting for this moment too long already and watching everyone walk before me so slowly made me want to scream, "hurry up!"

The wedding itself included a full mass, with traditional vows. But instead of "until death do you part," we both said, "I will honor you, cherish you, and love you all the days of my life." The priest's ending words were my favorite. After

"You may now kiss the bride," he said, "I would like to introduce to you, the newly married couple."

Jerry and I held hands as we walked out of the church towards the limo waiting to take us to the reception. In the limo, we opened a bottle of champagne and clinked our glasses.

"Sarah, I love you and always will for the rest of my life. Never did I think I would be a married man, and look at me now, a man who doesn't want to spend a minute without his wife by his side. May we always agree to disagree."

"Jerry, I have known for a while that I will love you and cherish every moment together for the rest of my life. We will grow old and gray together, my love."

Our first dance as husband and wife was to the song "Tonight I Celebrate My Love." As I clung to Jerry, I felt as though the world around me had stopped and we were the only two in existence. I knew everyone was watching us dance and there were people filming, but I didn't see any of it. All I saw was my husband. I had this overwhelming feeling that life couldn't get any better than this. During our dance, Jerry put his hand on my cheek, and I looked into his tearful eyes. He kissed me and held on tighter. When our song was over, Jerry wiped his eyes. I tried hard to hold back my tears, so my makeup wouldn't run.

After our first dance, we had the father-daughter and mother-son dance. My brother danced with me, and Jerry danced with his mom. The four of us danced to "Wind Beneath My Wings."

Our cake was beautiful with three tiers. Each layer was done in an octagon shape with white frosting, and an off-white basket weave draped down each side of the cake made with a different type of frosting. The contrast was beautiful. The baker had also coordinated with the florist to decorate the cake with white lilies and ivy that matched my bouquet.

A Soulmates Twin Flame

When it came time for the cake, I was nice. Jerry, not so much, I had to clean up some smeared frosting off my cheek. While the song played that said, "The bride kisses the groom, and then the groom kisses the bride", the DJ chimed in and said, "ok one more verse." He then sang with music "The groom kisses the DJ". Jerry, always the comedian, left me and ran over to kiss the DJ. They played the song "YMCA" and four of the men got up and pretended to be the Village People, with Jerry front and center, strutting his stuff.

The final picture that the photographer took was one of my favorites. He asked us to come outside and took a photo of our backs walking away holding hands as we started our new life together as husband and wife.

Our Wedding & Reception

Jerry and I had spent a good amount of money on our wedding so we did not plan an extravagant honeymoon. We were married, planned the wedding of our dreams and were now united under God. To me, that's what mattered.

We went back home after the wedding and opened all the cards. We had only been given one present to open.

"Alright baby let's start opening cards and see what we got," Jerry said.

"Okay, here's half for you to open," I said as I handed him a stack of cards.

"Look, the first card and there's a one hundred dollar bill. I hope we get more like this," he said with excitement.

"I got one with a fifty dollar bill. I know, not as lucky as your card, but we are just beginning," I replied.

Thanks to all the generous cash gifts from friends and family, we were taking a honeymoon road trip to Florida. Our first stop was at what sounded like a romantic place to spend the night.

"Sarah, don't go in the room yet, give me a second," Jerry said while he was getting a few things out of the car.

"Why not, I just want to see what it looks like," I said.

"Would you please just wait a second?"

"Okay, fine," I said as Jerry was walking over to me.

"Now we are going to enter the room." With a huge smile, he then picked me up.

"What are you doing? Are you kidding me? We don't have to do that threshold thing you know. I'm too heavy, ok you can put me down now!"

Our honeymoon suite was decorated nicely and would have been romantic with a heart-shaped hot tub in the middle, but cleanliness was an issue. We cleaned a little ourselves but did not use the hot tub. It didn't matter. We talked for hours over a few bottles of champagne and made love that night as husband and wife. We checked out the next morning and told them what we thought of their cleanliness.

We got back on the road and started driving again. We were headed back to Disney world for a few days. This trip we visited the Epcot theme park. We saw the parade of Worlds, walked through a few different countries, and went on the train ride that took you through the giant golf ball. The ride was boring, yet interesting at the same time.

That evening we had dinner in France; it was elegant and romantic. We were seated at a candlelit table and given menus. The server was hard to understand with his sharp French accent, and then we opened the menus. We looked at each other and laughed, the entire menu was written in French. Duh! When we tried to ask what some items were, we were still confused as we could barely understand his English. We placed our order for dinner and waited to see what would be served to us. Jerry enjoyed his meal. I, not so much. We had a blast the rest of the evening touring a few more countries and watching a firework show over the water as Disney was celebrating the new millennium.

The next day we went to a timeshare seminar for the sole purpose of receiving tickets to Universal Studios. Jerry and I saw this park being built last time in Florida and took a picture of me in front of the billboard for it and said, "we will be back when this opens." We were roller coaster junkies, and Universal Studios didn't disappoint us. The Twin Dragons gave the illusion of a head-on collision with its twin coaster. The Incredible Hulk coaster took us through a few tunnels under water and had some intense free-fall drops. Their park photographer offered us our photo in an Islands of Adventure frame, for a small fortune. Sure, we said. It was one of the few pictures from our honeymoon where we were together in the photo.

The next morning, we woke up early and went to Disney's Animal Kingdom. We took a safari ride through the jungle and saw many beautiful wild animals, a few came close to the vehicle we were in. I've never seen so many wild animals free roaming before.

The next day we started our journey back home. Before we left Florida, I made a call and booked us a room at the Poconos resort in Pennsylvania. I had wanted to go there but wasn't sure about money until the day we left.

When we arrived at the resort and checked in, I was excited about getting to our room, knowing it was going to be the most romantic night on our honeymoon. Our room had a large bed in the shape of a circle, with a vibrating option. We had a separate room with a fireplace, a heart shape hot tub and our own private triangular swimming pool enclosed in a separate glass room. It was funny to watch Jerry get in the pool as I was still sitting on our bed getting ready to join him. The resort gave us a bottle of champagne, flowers, and two t-shirts that read "Best of 2000." The shirts had a few of the most popular things happening that year, the last statement reading, *We got married*. We had a wonderful evening filled with romance and passion.

When our honeymoon was over, we were glad to be home. We missed our little girl.

Our Honeymoon

Sarah J Provost

Life, It Happens
Love is tender and kind

Isabelle was almost a year old, and money was tight. When my father passed away, he left a small inheritance and that allowed me to stay home that first year with Isabelle. I knew I had to find a day job with mother's hours and benefits. I had a friend who worked at a bank and put in a good word for me since I had no prior experience. I got the job, and Jerry's mom was now our daycare.

Jerry and I had date night every Tuesday. His mom would keep Isabelle overnight. We had a great time playing pool and joined a pool league. We loved our Tuesday nights, and competing against other teams was always fun.

In November 2000, we went to another concert. This time Jerry and I went to Rochester, New York, to see Styx, with opening bands Reo Speed Wagon, and Survivor. I knew more music than I thought.

"Eye of the tiger, everyone knows this song. Of course, they would open with their only hit," I said to Jerry.

"Okay, honey," he replied.

"Hey, I love this song. I thought Journey sang this?"

"You didn't know this was Survivor? You sing it all the time," he said while laughing at me.

"I know I sing it a lot, but come on, doesn't it sound like Journey?"

"No, it sounds like Survivor," Jerry said sarcastically.

"Oh shit! I thought Journey sang this one too," I said while singing.

A Soulmates Twin Flame

"Are you kidding me, you are too much." Jerry was rolling his eyes at me and laughing.

I had plenty of fun that night and Jerry said he had a great time with how much I made him laugh.

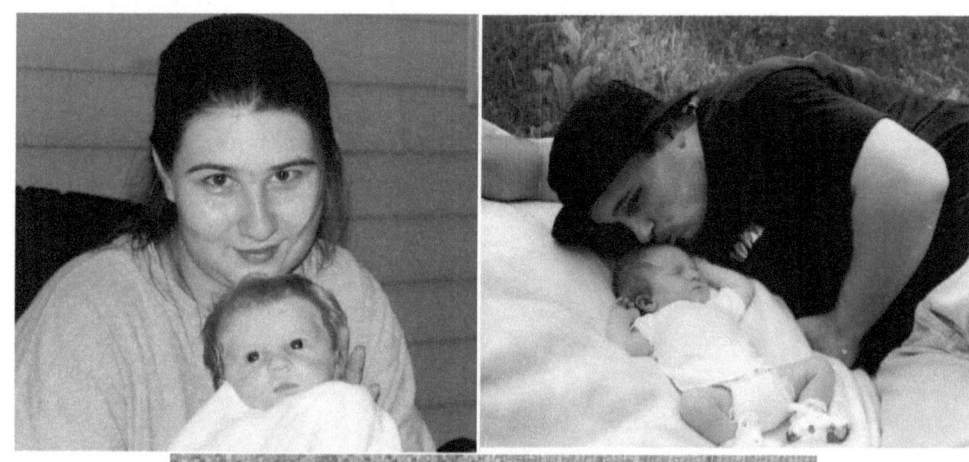

Our Little Girl

How fast she grows

Over the next few months, things seemed to be getting better financially, but that didn't last long. Jerry had worked nights at the restaurant and sometimes he would come home late, or worse, early in the morning. Once the night was done, they would all have a few beers. Well, sometimes turned into all the time. Jerry would stumble through the door anytime between 2:00 and 3:00 in the morning. Being my calm and humble self, I would ask him what he did all night and he would say that he had a few beers with friends, and I would say ok. I asked him one night to please just come home after work. That didn't happen. A few more months went by and I had had enough. We still had our Tuesday night pool league. He always had every Tuesday off. On those nights he would act like everything was hunky dory and he did no wrong any other day. Jerry stumbled through the door one evening, and I was waiting up for him like I did every night making sure he made it home ok.

"Jerry, I have had enough. I am done. All you do is work and drink. I don't understand why you don't want to see me or your daughter. She doesn't even know who you are anymore. If I am going to be alone and a single mother, then I am going to do it without you. You don't even make money anymore. You drink away your paycheck each week, and I struggle to keep everything paid by myself. Did you know the gas got shut off last week because I couldn't afford it? I had to call my mother for help so me and Isabelle could have hot water." I was angry, and I wanted him to know it.

"What is your problem tonight?" he replied.

"Are you serious, did you not hear anything I just said to you?" I was annoyed and all kinds of hurt.

"You're just jealous because you can't go out anymore and have to stay home to take care of a child," he replied, laughing.

"This so-called child was your idea in the first place. We are done, have a nice life!" I said to him, crying.

A Soulmates Twin Flame

I went upstairs to our bedroom hysterical, not understanding why he didn't miss us the way we missed him. It was something I couldn't comprehend. Don't get me wrong, there was also jealousy constantly flowing through me. We agreed to grow up and start a family. I felt like I was left holding the bag and being the one who had to be solely responsible for a child and paying the bills. I wanted to go out, have a few drinks, and some fun too, but it was not an option. After an hour Jerry came upstairs and laid next to me. I ignored him, fell asleep and was awoken by the alarm two hours later. I brought Isabelle to Jerry's mom that morning and called in sick to work. I lay back down next to Jerry that morning, watching him sleep. I thought to myself, *I love him so much, I can't leave him. I don't know what to do. This hurts so much every day, but not being with him would hurt even more. I am so confused.* These thoughts kept playing in my head. I fell asleep again. He woke up and then woke me up.

"Sarah get up, you're very late for work. Where is Isabelle?" Jerry asked.

"She's at your mom's, and I called in sick. After last night, I am in no shape to handle a day at work. Please leave me alone," I replied with disgust in my voice.

"I'm going to take a shower; can we please talk when I'm done?" Jerry asked politely.

"Fine," I said.

Jerry took his shower while I made us a pot of coffee. I had no idea what he wanted to talk about. I heard him loud and clear the previous night that he didn't care about me or Isabelle. It was now just a matter of who would pack and move out. As much as I didn't want to part ways and was so in love, I was not going to be treated that way.

"Sarah, please listen to me for a minute. I am sorry. I know I don't deserve your forgiveness, but I am asking anyway. I have been an inconsiderate asshole, I know. I thought about everything you said last night. I might have had a few too many, but I did listen, and I heard you. I love you and Isabelle very much. I don't know what I was thinking and why I drank so much. After work, I would have a beer and I thought about getting home to you guys. I would be handed a second beer, and then all thoughts were gone and I just wanted to keep drinking. I didn't know how to stop until I was forced to leave. Sarah, I don't know what else to say. I screwed up. Will you please talk to me and try to forgive me? I don't want to lose you or Isabelle."

"I don't know what to say. I am hurt. I love you more than you know, but I can't continue to live like this. It hurts too much," I said.

"Sarah, please give me one more chance. There will be no more drinking. I will not drink at all after work, I promise you that. It might have taken me awhile to realize but you mean more to me than anything ever has in my life. I love you, Sarah. I am sorry. One more chance, please?" Jerry's eyes were teary.

"One more chance. Don't for a second think that I won't pack our bags and be gone if this shit happens again. I certainly do love you, but I have my limits. Right now, I am hurt and confused. I don't understand how beer can make you forget about your family."

Jerry and I spent the rest of the day together cleaning the house and talking. We went out that evening to our weekly pool league and had fun. Jerry had a few beers, and I had a few drinks as well, then we both had sodas. We didn't make love that night, but we had sex. It was satisfying on some level, but in no way reached my soul. Old habits were hard to break, and Jerry had been drinking heavily for many years.

Jerry went to work the next day as did I. I waited for him to get home. To my surprise, he was home at nine-thirty and Isabelle was still awake. I was dumbfounded, to say the least. I couldn't believe that an alcoholic could stop drinking cold turkey. It had to be a fluke. Another week went by, and each night he came home, always around nine-thirty. Each night after he got home, I waited to hear him complain or something. He never said anything about a beer and always had a smile, and we were back to our loving playful nature. I would still feel hurt periodically when I would think about it over the next few weeks. A few times I felt so angry and hurt and didn't want to even look at him when I thought about it too much. Did it really have to go that far, where I had to point out "Hey, dumbass you have a wife and a daughter who love you. If you don't smarten up you're gonna lose them." It took me some time, but I was able to slowly get over it and diminish those thoughts.

Once again things seemed to be on the right track. It had been a little over a month since Jerry had quit drinking. We were spending the evenings as a family. Isabelle and I got a surprise one day. Jerry was pulling into the driveway and it was only late afternoon. I was shocked.

"Hey, baby! How are my girls?" Jerry asked with a smile.

"We are good, even better now, but I'm confused. How did you manage to leave early on a Saturday night?" I asked.

"It wasn't easy, but I got everything prepped and ready and showed the line cooks everything they needed to do to get through the night. Then I said I wasn't feeling good and left. I wanted to surprise my two ladies and have more than just an hour with Isabelle tonight," he explained.

"This is awesome, a Saturday night, and we are all home together!" I said excitedly.

"Did you guys have dinner yet?" Jerry asked.

"Look, there's a cop in the driveway sitting in his car. I bet he's here for the loser next door," I said.

I closed the blinds and we started talking about dinner when the doorbell rang. I opened the door and it was the police officer. My first thought was to tell him the loser is next door, until he mentioned a name.

"Good evening ma'am, I am looking to speak with Gerard Provost," the officer said very politely.

"Hi sir, how are you? I'm Gerard, what can I help you with this evening?" Jerry said to the officer.

"Yes, sir. I am here serving an arrest warrant. There is a warrant out for your arrest pertaining to missed jury duty. I need to take you into custody. Your wife can come down to the station in a few hours and pick you up. Ma'am, you need to call first," the officer explained to us.

The tears started to flow as Jerry was taken into custody. It took me almost an hour to calm down, and then I made the call so I could go and pick him up. To my surprise, he wasn't going anywhere. The lady at the Police station told me that there were two other warrants out for Jerry's arrest and to be at the courthouse Monday morning with a lawyer. I was sick to my stomach. Just when I had thought things were going well financially and happily, shit hit the fan again. I called Jerry's mom to tell her what happened, and she gave me the number to a criminal lawyer that I could call on a Sunday. I then sucked it up and called my mom for help with money. I did not want to ask for her help, but I didn't know who else to call. What was she going to think? I just asked her for money two months ago to pay a bill. I was scared to tell her; I didn't want to listen to any lectures. The next day, I went to mom's, borrowed money, and was all set to meet the lawyer Monday morning at the courthouse. Throughout that day I had to listen to friends and family tell me that my husband was no good for me, couldn't keep a job, and worse. I tried to explain that I loved him, but no one cared about that. "You should at least be mad at him," they would say, and I would ask why? Why would I be mad at him? I was upset at the situation, but not Jerry. We all make mistakes. He made these mistakes a long time ago, before I was part of his life. No one understood me, or what mattered to me, and it sure wasn't money like they all thought it should have been. That was the longest weekend of my life.

A Soulmates Twin Flame

In addition to missing jury duty, Jerry had also failed to attend Anger Management classes stemming from an earlier incident. Then there was a second warrant for illegal drugs— mushrooms and marijuana— that he and his friends got caught with before he moved in with me all those years ago. After a full day of court hopping, all charges were dropped, thanks to the lawyer who knew his way around the legal system.

Jerry and I went home after that and asked his mom if she could keep Isabelle, so we could have the night alone together. We celebrated that he was home and had a good evening. Jerry was a no call/no show at his job for two days and was fired. I was glad and looked at that as a blessing in disguise. I never liked where he worked. In the back of my mind I was scared that he would go back to drinking. Even though he was coming home every night, I would say to myself, "Is this the night he decides to have a beer?" Him losing the job was like a weight lifted from my shoulders. I had no doubts that he would find another job quickly. I think I had more confidence in him than he did in himself.

More Surprises

Time for Something New
Jobs, Vacations and Problems

After searching for a few weeks, Jerry found a new job. He was hired by the Friendly's Corporation as a General Manager. This turned out to be his best opportunity yet with a great salary, bonuses, and good medical benefits. There was training for this new job that was a week long. He was supposed to be away for a week, but we were not having that. When Jerry started the training, he left the hotel each night and drove home to sleep next to me. He woke up each morning at 4:00 to head back to training.

With this new Job, Jerry made the schedule. He worked a lot but made sure he still had a few evenings with his family each week. Once or twice a week Isabelle and I would go out to eat at Friendly's so we could see him before Isabelle went to bed. I liked it because I didn't have to cook, and it was always free. Her favorite part was when daddy would take her in the kitchen, and she got to make her own sundae.

On the days we both worked the same hours, we'd cook dinner together and Jerry enjoyed playing with Isabelle. Often Isabelle would fall asleep somewhere other than her bed. On those nights Jerry and I would play in her room. She had a toy that we both had fun with, a blow up ball pit filled with hundreds of plastic balls.

Jerry and I spent hours playing tennis and volleyball in her room, hitting the balls back and forth, without letting them hit the ground. If someone missed, the other one got a point. The winner received whatever they desired from the loser. Sometimes we would just see who was faster at throwing the balls to hit the other person until they couldn't take it anymore. We would lose track of time and realize that we spent the last three hours being kids and laughing.

Sarah J Provost

It had been a while since we had a fun adult adventure outside the house other than our Tuesday night pool league, so we planned a camping trip with another couple to a place called "Thousand Acre Swamp". We had gone fishing in our canoe there many times, and every time we were out on the water, we would look at the island in the center. From what we could see it looked like mostly woods, but there were enough open areas to set up a few tents. Jerry said it would be fun to go camping there, and I agreed, even though it looked isolated and creepy.

We canoed over to the island on a sunny afternoon and found a spot where we could set up two tents and build a campfire. As it was getting close to dusk we got a fire going and then cooked dinner. The two men went to collect more firewood while the girls waited by the camp. We were all a little scared as we were on an island surrounded by a swamp in which we had no idea what lurked in that water other than large bass. There was not another person to be found on that island. We heard so many noises and sounds that night, most unrecognizable. We told ghost stories around the fire trying to incorporate the sounds we heard into the stories. Jerry was the best storyteller among us; he had us scared and sounded so believable. We collected enough firewood to keep it going all night and for some light.

We were all a little tired and got ready to set up our tents.

"Jerry let's get the tent set up," I said.

"Ok, I'll be right there," he replied.

I started unpacking the tent, pulled everything out of the bag and made a shocking discovery.

"Jerry, we have a problem," I said in my astronaut voice.

"You're trying to be silly and laughing. What did we forget this time?" he asked.

A Soulmates Twin Flame

"Honey, I hate to break it to you but there are no tent poles."

"Are you kidding me? What the fuck!"

"I don't know why they're not in there," I said. "Shit just seems to vanish at our house."

"Alright, let me think for a minute," Jerry said.

"You know what, we're just gonna use the oars from the canoe to hold up a spot in the center so at least we will have a little shelter," he said.

"Sounds good to me. Look at it this way, that's easier than those stupid tent pole anyways," I replied.

We set up our tent and got in, immediately dislodging an oar. On the second try, it was several seconds before the other oar fell. Jerry was starting to get frustrated. "Third time's a charm!" I promised, and fortunately I was right. The problem then was that we were smothered by the tent in all but a tiny spot. We didn't sleep much, and while trying to get it on in our tiny little area, we knocked down an oar. The sun came up, and we packed our stuff to get ready to leave. That was the easiest time we ever had taking the tent down.

Over the next year, Jerry got to spend plenty of time with his daughter and me too. He would take to her to different parks because she loved the swings. One day Jerry took her to the air force base. She loved it. Her favorite part was standing in front of the tires as they were so much bigger than her. Daddy played more than mommy and she loved it. He was up for anything. Jerry had just as much fun on Easter egg hunts and hayrides as she did.

Later that year, Jerry woke up in tears one morning. He said that he had a lot of stomach pain. He ran to the bathroom and vomited. After a few minutes, he said the pain was horrible and had trouble standing up. We went straight to the Emergency Room where we learned he had kidney stones. He was given morphine for the pain.

"Sarah, I am so sorry. I will never put you through that again. I am so sorry. I had no idea," Jerry said with sympathy as he had tears in his eyes and seemed a bit delusional.

"It's ok honey," I responded. What was he talking about? I had no idea.

"Sarah, I'm sorry, I'm so sorry, I love you!" he said.

"Jerry it's ok, don't even worry about," I said again trying not laugh at him.

The nurse had overheard him apologizing and explained that one of the doctors told Jerry that having a kidney stone was the closest a man would get to understanding labor pains. The nurse told me I could take Jerry home but to stay with him because of the amount of morphine he'd been given. I said not a problem, as this was a laugh your ass off at Jerry day for me. She said the stone would pass in his urine within a day. Jerry continued apologizing until the morphine high wore off. Later that night, Jerry passed the stone which was closer in size to a grain of sand. Jerry was pissed.

"That tiny little thing caused that much pain? That's bullshit," he said.

Around this time, Jerry and I traded in our beat up old truck and bought a new one. After our Tuesday night pool league one week, we decided to go four wheeling and knew exactly where to go. I was having a great time, and then we got stuck.

"Are you kidding me, what the fuck! I just wanted to have a little fun," Jerry said. We were stuck in a deep mud rut, and Jerry was pissed.

"Look on the bright side, at least we had fun," I said back to him in hopes that maybe I could get the smile back.

"It doesn't matter what I do, 'Murphy' is by my side every day, and I'm tired of it!"

He assessed the situation for a moment, staring at the mess with his hands on his hips.

"Sarah, please get into the driver's seat. I knew I should have bought a winch. You see that tree? That would have been our way to pull out of here."

"Alright, what do you want to try, forward or reverse?" I asked.

"Try reverse while I push," he said after he found a few things to wedge under the tires.

We tried a few times in reverse and then we tried going forward and had no luck either way.

"Ah baby, this isn't working, and you're a mess," I said, laughing. He was covered in mud.

"Do you not think I realize that already!" Jerry yelled as he rolled his eyes at me.

"Well, you know what, it's not my fault, so you don't have to be such an asshole," I said.

"I'm going to start walking and find a payphone. You can wait here in the truck if you want. "

"I don't think so, not alone. Its two o'clock in the morning, very dark and nothing but trees outside this field."

We walked for about an hour until we got to the road. We found a payphone half a mile down the street. We used the torn up phone directory, and after many calls, we found someone who was willing to come and pull us out. Jerry and I drove home after that and we both laughed because it had been a lot of fun.

"I'll do Isabelle's bath, and you can do the truck bath tomorrow" I said. He argued for a second then said, "Fine, dear," in his sarcastic anything-for-you-tone.

Sarah J Provost

Jerry and I still enjoyed our road trips and adventures, except now they were shorter, closer to home and there were three of us. Isabelle enjoyed going for car rides too. We took her to the Boston aquarium and spent most of our time around the penguins, Isabelle's favorite. We would walk and look at other fish, and she would ask, "Can we go see the penguins now?" We'd look at one fish tank, and then penguins; we'd see something else and then back to penguins. That went on the entire day. I grew tired of seeing penguins.

We took Isabelle to the beach in Southern Connecticut another day. The ride was two and a half hours one way. She was so excited, but when it was time to go in the water, she freaked out and started screaming. We only stayed another ten minutes after that, as she just kept crying and saying she wanted to go home. We drove another two and a half hours back home after being at the beach for less than an hour.

July of 2002, we went camping at Lake Champlain, a spontaneous trip as we needed to get away. Isabelle, who had turned three a few months prior, didn't understand what had happened that day. She had a friend who lived next door and they had spent the day swimming together with another little girl in a kiddie pool. A horrible accident happened, and her friend drowned in the kiddie pool that was only filled with four inches of water. Lake Champlain was five hours away and Jerry and I thought a long ride would be good for her and help all of us relax.

We arrived, found my mother and her husband, and camped with them for the evening. Isabelle seemed to forget about everything that had happened and laughed and smiled. She helped daddy build a campfire, and we all told funny stories. Her favorite part of the evening was gathering sticks and roasting marshmallows with daddy. We used this trip to teach Isabelle how to use a camera as well. Jerry and I don't have many pictures together, so she became our little photographer. When the photos were developed, we showed her. She was so proud of herself and asked if daddy would buy her a camera of her own. We all struggled to understand what happened to Isabelle's friend, and why.

Camping at Lake Champlain

A Soulmates Twin Flame

Ready or Not

Love is passionate and honest

It was the summer of 2003, Isabelle had just turned four years old, and I had an all-too-familiar feeling. I thought to myself *"I think we are going to have another child."* I was nervous, yet I was happy. I didn't know if I was ready for a second child, but at the same time thought if we did have more children I didn't want there to be a huge age gap between them. I told Jerry my symptoms, and he was ecstatic.

"Oh my God, are you kidding me. Sarah you're pregnant!" Jerry said loudly with a huge smile.

"Okay, don't get your hopes up yet, those are my symptoms. For all we know I could just be sick."

"I'll go right now and buy a pregnancy test. Baby, I love you!"

Jerry left the house and went to the store. I was now feeling anxious and overjoyed. The nervous feeling was gone. His excitement and happiness were contagious. He got back home, and the test confirmed my suspicions. We were having another child. We celebrated and told Isabelle. She said she couldn't wait to have a sister. We had to break the news to her that it was possible she might get a brother, but she was holding out for a sister.

A few months later, when I started to feel better Jerry and I planned a romantic getaway before the addition to our family arrived. We made reservations again at the Poconos Resort in Pennsylvania. Jerry and I stayed in a room very similar to the last time we were there. We enjoyed having our own private swimming pool. That evening we had dinner in the dining room with all the other couples. During dinner, they took a photo of us, and I purchased the memento. The background of the photo was a wine glass and our faces in the center and at the bottom were red roses and the year.

Our romantic night away

Sarah J Provost

After dinner, we saw a comedy show. Being a lover's resort, all the jokes revolved around relationships and sex. We had a lot of laughs that night during the show and afterwards enjoyed our private pool and hot tub.

That night before we went to bed, Jerry reached in his pocket and pulled out a pair of beautiful earrings to celebrate our second child. They had the birthstone for the month he/she was going to be born and two diamonds above it. I loved it! When I was pregnant with Isabelle Jerry bought me a mother's ring that had her birthstone and diamonds along with the earrings that matched the ring. I can't explain how happy I felt that evening and the love between us.

Jerry and I knew that we had to find a new place to live. The house we were in was a two bedroom and we needed a three bedroom. In November of 2003, my brother had called us and said he was moving. He knew we were looking to move into a bigger house and offered to sell his house to us. Jerry had a great job with the Friendly's Corporation and my brother gave us the equity he accrued in the house, so we didn't need to come up with a down payment. Jerry was approved for the mortgage.

After we moved in, we knew the first thing we wanted to do was get a wood stove to help with the heat. The master bedroom was originally a breezeway leading to the garage, and the heat was an extension from the original system. The bedroom never got warm. We used space heaters until we found a wood stove. We cut two large windows into the wall on the garage side and the stove was in the garage. Our bedroom was now warmer, but any slight variations in the wood, our bedroom would fill with smoke. Many times, our clothes smelled like we had spent the day around the campfire, when in fact we just pulled them out of the drawer or closet.

Jerry being a typical big baby, got a splinter one day and asked Dr. Sarah to fix it. He would call me Dr. Sarah, or Nurse Sarah when he had a problem that involved his own blood. He said it hurt a lot and couldn't get it out without having to remove some skin first. I lead him into the bathroom and went to work. I was glad he didn't get it out himself, or I might have found him passed out somewhere. This was a splinter towards the skin and turned into a chunk of wood deeper into his palm. When I first pulled it out, it wasn't just bleeding, but squirting blood. I told him not to look and got him all fixed up. He said it felt much better and I got a kiss.

Jerry and I finally finished setting up our new house and getting the nursery ready. We were in the basement one evening doing laundry and talking.

"You know we have all this space down here with just a washer and dryer, why don't we turn it into something," Jerry said.

"I don't know what we would turn it into. Did you have an idea or something?" I asked.

"I was thinking, we could turn half into a playroom for Isabelle and get those foam colored puzzle things as her floor, and then for our half, we could get a pool table. With two kids soon, you know there are going to be fewer adventures out for us."

"I would love a pool table, but there's no way we can afford that, so we're not getting one," I stated.

"No shit, we can't afford it. I'm not a moron. It's Christmas soon. You were there when my mom asked if there was anything we wanted for Christmas that we would like or need for the house," Jerry replied.

"Are you really going to ask her for a pool table?"

"Why not, she said anything."

Jerry and I ended up getting the pool table, and we set up a stereo. We could play pool just the two of us all night. We'd make silly bets. We were lame when it came to what the winner got. It was almost always the loser was the slave to the winner for one evening. I was usually the loser, but not always. We would say "ok the first one to win five games." When he won five games, I would say, "I still want to play, how about the first one to win seven games." We had a great time in our basement.

Jerry woke up one morning and scared the crap out of me.

"It's a boy, and his name is Brendan," Jerry practically screamed as he sat up in bed and woke me up.

"I'm tired and I was sleeping, a little loud don't you think? Can you please check if Isabelle is awake?" I whispered.

"Baby listen to me, please! It's a boy, I know it. His name is Brendan," he said again.

"Ok, so you think we're having a boy. I hope your right, I'd love a boy. Can I please go back to sleep for a little while?"

"You don't understand, I know it's a boy. I just know, I have this feeling. I can't explain it right now, I just know. Can you believe it, baby, we're having a boy!"

"I love you! We'll find out in a few days. I guess it's time to get up."

A few days later we went back to the doctor and found out that we were having a boy. I told Jerry that the name Brendan was perfect, and I loved it. He said to me "I told you, I just had this feeling, and I knew."

As bad luck would have it, Jerry lost his job and our medical benefits a month before Brendan was born. We hadn't been in our new house for very long and had to try and figure out a way to make the payments. I had just quit my job at the bank because I wanted to stay home with Brendan for the first year. Jerry received unemployment, but it wasn't as much as he was making while working. I was scared and nervous. Brendan was coming whether we were financially ready or not. Within two weeks Jerry had found a job under the table cleaning restaurant hood and exhaust systems. I felt a little relief but was still scared.

A Soulmates Twin Flame

Brendan's due date had arrived. It was one o'clock in the morning when my water broke. I woke up Jerry, he got Isabelle and called his mom. Isabelle ran out of her room and started talking to mommy's belly.

"It's about time, little brother, I've been waiting for you to get here," she said with a huge smile.

It took less than ten minutes to get out the door, and by that time I was in extreme pain. We headed to the hospital. The pain kept increasing and ran into the same problem as we did with first child. I was given the same drug and again told to walk around to help my body. They constantly checked Brendan's heartbeat while I was on that medication. The nurse was doing a heartbeat check and gave us a scare.

"Sarah, we need to check his heartbeat again," the nurse said.

"Okay," I replied as I could barely speak because of the pain, and we had already done this twice thus far that evening.

"Sarah, try to be still, please. I'm having a hard time hearing his heartbeat," the nurse said with hesitation in her voice.

"What? What do you mean? What? Are you not hearing a heartbeat? Is it just a quiet heartbeat? This is taking too long! Do you hear Brendan's heartbeat?" Jerry's anxiety was making me nervous.

"Sir, give me just a minute, I'm listening," she said to Jerry.

"Did you hear Brendan's heartbeat?" This question came a split second after she asked for a minute.

A second nurse checked and failed to hear the heartbeat. Jerry and I were both in a panic.

"What's going on? Please tell me you hear his heartbeat," Jerry said. I could hear the fear in his voice.

The first nurse was again listening.

"His heart is beating just fine and is very strong," the nurse said to us

"Oh my God, Thank you, God!" Jerry said with a huge sigh of relief.

I don't know if I have ever been more scared in my life than I was that night. The whole incidence was less than two minutes, but it felt like a lifetime. The nurse could not answer our question when we asked if Brendan's heart had possibly stopped beating momentarily or if it was just a matter of location while she was listening, or possibly equipment malfunction. She told us that she wasn't sure what had happened. It wasn't long after that when I received the epidural. I finally had some relief, but not for long. The time to push had arrived very fast with the help of that medication. It took fifteen minutes from the first push to the last and Brendan was born. 9:15 am Sunday, February 1st. We had a healthy baby boy!

Brendan was born on Super Bowl Sunday when the Patriots won over the Carolina Panthers. We received many gifts that day, and all were Super Bowl-related.

While Jerry was holding Brendan, we talked about the days both kids were born.

"You know what's weird. Both kids were born on the date the doctor gave at the beginning of each pregnancy. Not a day before or after, but the exact date. What are the chances?" Jerry said, still smiling and holding Brendan.

"I don't know honey, but you might have played a part in Isabelle being born on her due date. Remember the boat ride, that might have had something to do with it," I said.

Brendan was such a happy baby. Jerry and I were not sure if he even knew how to cry. He was either smiling and laughing or just calm and happy when he wasn't sleeping. With child number two, we learned how important a schedule was for a newborn. After the first few months, Brendan was sleeping from seven to seven with two scheduled naps during the day.

Jerry had been working almost every day. When Brendan was three months old, Jerry and I had a whole day together.

"After dinner, let's get a movie, a bottle of wine and just relax. It's been a while since we have been able to watch a whole movie uninterrupted," I said.

He agreed and said it sounded like a great idea. The phone rang shortly after that and it was a friend asking Jerry if he wanted to go fishing.

"Hey honey, it's Mark on the phone. Do you mind if I go fishing for a few hours? It's only 11:00 am, I'll be back before dinner. You can call my mom and have her visit with the kids while you go get us the movie and a bottle of wine," Jerry said.

"I don't know, I guess I don't mind. Promise me you will be home before five o'clock tonight, so we can make dinner together and watch our movie," I said. I knew how Jerry had a habit of forgetting about time when he had a fishing pole in his hands.

"Baby don't worry, I will be home. I can't wait to snuggle with you tonight after we put the kids to bed."

Jerry was out the door to go fishing within ten minutes after he hung up the phone. I called his mom and asked her to stay with the kids for an hour. I needed to do this simple errand alone for some quiet time. I kept looking at the clock. Five o'clock and no Jerry. Another hour went by and still no call, no show. After another hour, I called his friend's cell phone and asked to talk to Jerry. He answered the phone like he was all smiles and not a care in the world.

"Hi baby, how's my girl? I know it's after seven and, yes, I'm still on the water. We're having a great time, catching a lot of fish and talking," Jerry said.

"Really, you're still there? I would have at least expected you to say you were driving home, since your fishing spot is an hour away," I could barely speak because I had become hysterical crying.

"Sarah, please, I'm sorry, stop crying, baby. I love you!"

"I did everything I said I was going to do. Your mom sat with the kids, I went and got us a bottle of wine and a movie and have been waiting for you," I said to him, still crying while I heard him tell his friend that they had to leave immediately, and he was now in the dog house.

"Honey, please stop crying. We are almost back to shore, and we are leaving. I love you. I will be home soon."

Jerry finally walked through the door a little after nine o'clock that night. I never stopped crying after we hung up. Jerry also knew that I was dealing with some crazy emotions and deep sadness after giving birth to Brendan. This was new for both of us. I never felt any of that with our daughter. He sat down next to me on the couch and held me in his arms until I was calm enough to talk, and I pulled away from him.

"Jerry, I am so hurt. I thought you wanted to spend the night with me. I don't understand, you love me. I want to be with you, why don't you want to be with me? I don't understand. I need you, more now than ever. I tried to tell myself that you were just out fishing with a friend and stop being so hurt. Yes, I know I was the one that told you to go fishing but you know I'm struggling with whatever these emotions are. It's new to me, and you knew this. You should have just done what you said and been here when you said. It's not that difficult." I was crying again.

"Sarah, calm down. I do love you, you know this. Your right, I might not feel what you're talking about, but I did know about it. It's actually quite frustrating at times how you fall apart at absolutely nothing. That's not the calm, carefree, happy-go-lucky girl that I know. Where did she go? I needed this fishing trip. I sometimes don't know what to say to you, everything makes you cry. It's rather annoying. You're still crying and can barely talk. Maybe we should call a doctor," Jerry said. His happy tone was gone.

"I don't need a doctor, I just need you. I'm trying just give me time."

"If you don't start to feel better or feel like your old self in a few weeks, I really think we need to call a doctor and maybe see about getting you some help. Why don't you go lie down and try to get some sleep."

"Okay, will you please lie down with me and hold me?"

We laid down together and fell asleep. I was so hurt, I felt like my heart had been ripped out of my chest that night. It was awful. The hurt was so overwhelming that I wasn't capable of being mad. It felt like my world came crashing down and I was helpless. I will never forget that night. I had cried a lot over many things those first months after Brendan was born. They were simple things, like forgetting something that we needed at the store. It would send me into this depression state with uncontrollable crying. Once calm, I would say to myself, "Sarah that's not you, don't let that happen again, or he's gonna run for the hills." Jerry never went running. There were times he would get so irritated and go outside alone and tell me he just needed a minute. It was only a few more weeks that I went through some crazy emotional outbursts, and we both noticed that I was back to my happy self. Thank goodness it was over. I felt relief that I thought it was finally over and scared at the same time wondering if something would set it off again.

The doctor called it postpartum depression and said some women need help, for others it just fades away, and for some, they don't experience any emotional changes. I will say though, I don't know how much more Jerry would have been able to handle. He was all I wanted at that time. I followed him around and always asked him to hug me. I was always affectionate, but this was over anyone's limits. This late home fishing incident hurt me more than his drinking days.

    A year after Brendan was born, Jerry was given an opportunity to buy the company he had been working for. We didn't have any money, so we talked with my mom and asked if her husband wanted to be partners with Jerry. They both liked the idea. She took out a loan and bought the business. They cleaned many restaurants from Maine down to Maryland. Most locations were within two hours of our home. The nights Jerry didn't get home until early morning, I would wait up, and we would sleep when the kids did. I wasn't comfortable getting into bed without my husband.

And then there was four

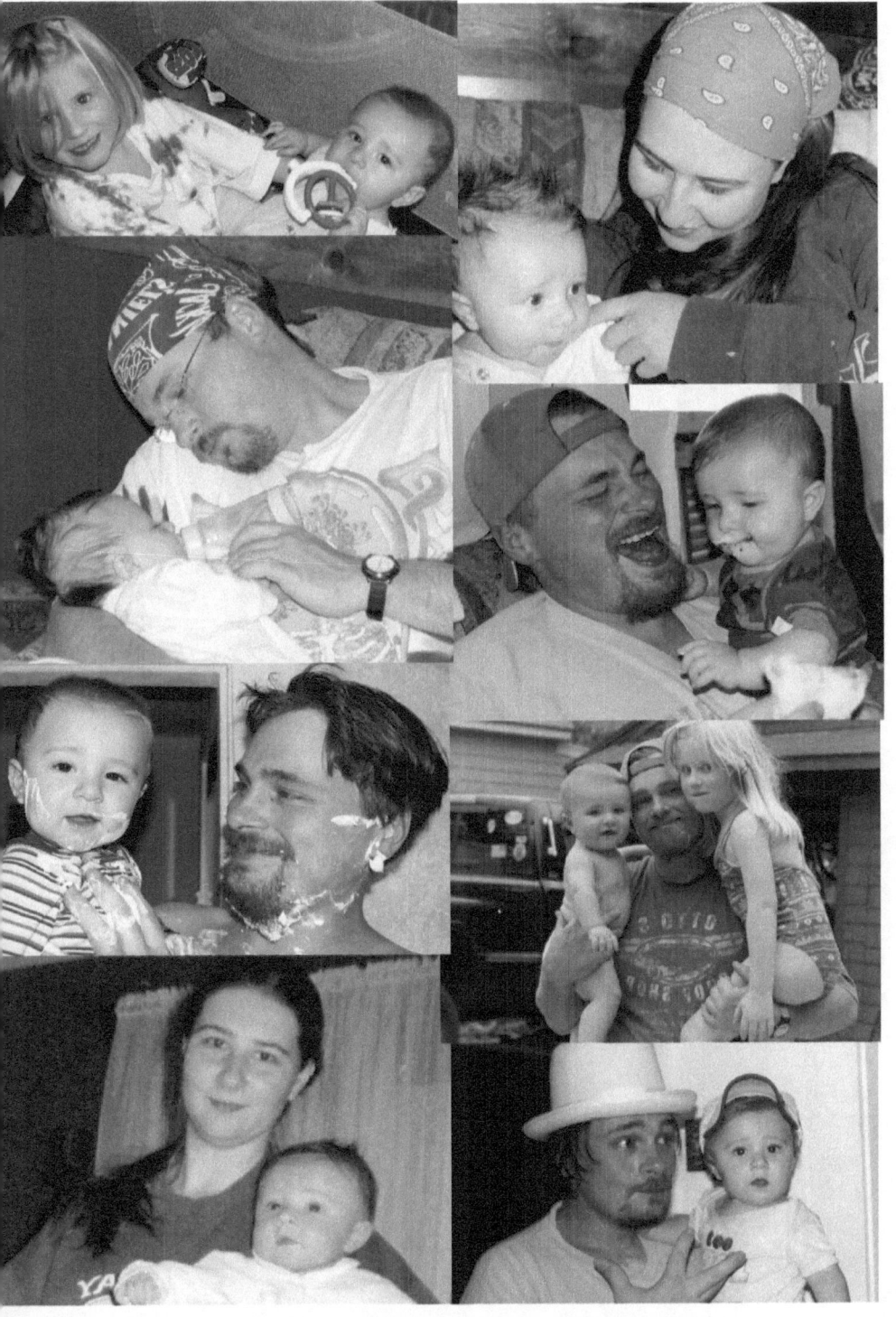

Where did the time go

A Soulmates Twin Flame

Big Changes and Fun
Going with the flow

A couple of months had gone by since Jerry turned co-owner of the new business. We were still struggling financially. Corporations paid once every few months and sent one large check for all the cleanings they had done. I had a job as a waitress, but this place was nothing to brag about money wise. We were many payments behind on the mortgage. My mother made a few payments for us to keep our heads above water, but Jerry and I knew we had to do something before we lost the house.

My mother had told us she was leaving her job and wanted to move to North Carolina and asked if we wanted to move too. They vacationed there many times and thought it was the perfect place to live. The business would have more potential as the largest chain we cleaned for had locations all the way down to Florida. We said sure, why not.

We contacted a realtor. She met with us and told us what we needed to do to the house to raise its value and get it ready for the market. She would come back in a month to list the house. Jerry and I rushed to get everything done.

Then Brendan got sick. Brendan never cried. He had multiple ear infections over the last year, but that was the only time he cried. After the first two infections, we learned that if he cried, he needed ear drops. Any other time he was full of laughter and smiles. This particular time, he had a high fever and the medicine didn't help. We brought him to the doctor thinking maybe some type of severe ear infection. The doctor examined Brendan and confirmed the high fever but couldn't find anything wrong and said there was no ear infection. He said he might just be battling a cold. They drew his blood before they sent us home that morning.

That afternoon, during a meeting with the realtor, the nurse called about Brendan's blood work. Something was wrong with his blood, and we were to take him straight to the hospital. Brendan was put through many tests and x-rays, but everything came back negative. We had no idea what was wrong, and his fever continued to rise. The doctor was concerned and recommended a high dose shot of antibiotics. We signed the consent form, and I held my baby boy as they gave him a shot in his upper leg. We were told to sit with him in the waiting area. He needed to be monitored in case of a possible reaction.

A little over an hour went by, and Brendan laughed. I broke out into tears of joy, as it had been days since I had heard his sweet laughter. The last four days all he had done was cry and sleep. Jerry ran to the nurse's desk, and they checked him again. He was now awake and laughing, and he asked for his juice. He no longer had a fever and they sent us home. We were told to monitor him closely in case the fever came back or he had a late reaction from the antibiotics. Brendan slept in our bed the next two nights, and he had no problems. We had a follow-up visit at the pediatrician and were informed that they were sorry but couldn't tell us what happened or what caused his illness. This scare will always be a mystery.

Jerry and I discussed having more children. I said I was happy that we had our boy and girl, and our family of four was perfect. He agreed. I did not want to be on birth control any longer, so we looked for a place for Jerry to get a vasectomy. After three places saying they didn't do that any longer, I took that as a sign and said, "Ok, I can have my tubes tied." I called the next day and scheduled a visit at my OBGYN to have the procedure done. Not long after that, surgery was scheduled, everything went well, and I didn't have to worry about birth control any longer.

It was August of 2005 when we made our way to North Carolina. Jerry and Isabelle drove, and Brendan and I flew in two days later. When Brendan and I arrived, Jerry and Isabelle were at our new house waiting for us. Jerry had found

A Soulmates Twin Flame

a nice quiet place to rent with a few acres of land when he moved my mom down a month prior. Our new home was in Shallotte. The location was perfect, but the house was a little small. We had sold a lot before the move, but still had contents from a house with an attic, a garage, and a basement. We somehow managed to fit all of it into a doublewide. We spent the first couple of weeks unpacking and frequently visiting the beach.

Early beach days in North Carolina

A Soulmates Twin Flame

When all the unpacking was done, we noticed that we didn't have many wall decorations, just the one from our very first apartment, a framed poster of the Great Smokey Mountains. We had wanted to take a trip there someday. This poster hung in every place we lived together. We would look at it and say, "one day we will get there."

We would hang that one, but we needed more, and I had to have Jerry's help. This is where it gets funny. I am smart and great at many things, but I am terrible at decorating, color matching, or anything like that. Thank goodness Jerry did not share my deficiencies.

"Jerry, come here I want you to see this. I think this would look great above the couch," I yelled to him from across the aisle.

"What did you find baby?"

"Okay, what do you think of these two pictures above the couch?" I asked.

"You know how much I love you, right?" He smiled at me.

"Yes, go on"

"Sarah, Sarah, Sarah, what I am going to do with you? Look, honey, you see the main colors here, you know my favorite color is purple, but this next to the green frame you picked out is not going to work. The new walls are red. I love your whole rainbow idea, I really do, but let's save that for our bedroom. I also see the curtains you picked out. What room are those for?"

"I thought they would look good in the front living room windows."

"They wouldn't look bad, but you're the one who complains about darkness in the house, so I have to say that's a no. The walls are such a deep dark red, that it would make it too dark, even when they're opened."

"Alright, well what did you find?" I asked.

Jerry showed me a few decorations that he thought would look good, and they were lighter, more neutral tones that actually helped to lighten the room. We did buy a few bright colored things for the bedroom. He really loved the rainbow idea but knew the living room wasn't the right place for it.

What's funny about our red walls is that the first apartment we rented together had red walls throughout. The first house we bought together had all red walls. The first home in a new state had all red walls. I don't know if together we were drawn to red or if they are calling to us, but either way, neither of us had ever lived somewhere with red walls until we got together as a couple.

Jerry began scheduling his first cleaning trip a few weeks after we moved. They would start in the North and work their way down the coast back home. The whole trip took about two weeks and was done every three months. Wow were those long weeks for me and the kids. We missed him! This was only the second time that we didn't go to bed together. We did talk multiple times a day and did phone sexting. Jerry also had a full-time job delivering doors and windows for a construction company when he wasn't on his trips.

In December of 2005, I had started a job with the electric company. I was excited that we were both working, and I was able to get benefits for our family. We then found a daycare for Brendan. As history repeats itself, Jerry's job with the construction company didn't last very long. Summer of 2006, Jerry was fired. We took Brendan out of daycare and he stayed home with Daddy. I say everything happens for a reason, and Brendan's daycare experience was not a good one, so daddy being home worked out. I was called from work many times when Brendan had even the slightest cough. There was one afternoon that I picked him up, and he was crying. I was told that he had been crying most of the day, and then they showed me his leg. He was bitten by another child. When I saw his leg, I was furious. I could see the teeth marks and he was swollen. They told me since it didn't look like the skin was broken, they didn't deem it necessary to call anyone. I brought him home and called in sick to work the next day trying to figure out what we could do. The next day I had to bring him back to daycare and spent some time talking to them that morning. It was that day that Jerry came home while I was at lunch and told me he got fired. I was not unhappy, as that solved my worries about Brendan. I felt like a weight was again lifted from my shoulders and didn't have to go to work worrying every day.

One beautiful fall afternoon we were all in the yard raking and cleaning. I grabbed our video camera while Jerry played with the kids in the leaf piles. I had fun videotaping their leaf fights. After the leaves were scattered back everywhere, Isabelle called to her father to chase her.

"Hey daddy, bet you can't catch me," Isabelle yelled from the other side of the yard.

"I'm done playing, you're being a crybaby about a few leaves in your hair," Jerry responded while trying to get the rake back from Brendan.

"C'mon daddy, chase me!"

"Not right now Isabelle, I'm trying to clean up all these leaves."

"Daddy, I'm ready!" Isabelle said in her cute little puppy dog voice.

"Ok, fine. You better start running."

As the two of them started running, Jerry was catching up to her quickly and made a sharp cut while running around a tree. He immediately stopped running and fell to the ground. He got up and said, "I'm done," and limped towards the house. Isabelle looked directly into the camera and said,

"Daddy is a loser! Daddy is a loser! I won."

We later found out that Jerry tore the ACL in his knee. When we watched the video, he put a sticker on it and labeled it 'Daddy makes a boo-boo'.

I have always thought my husband was a good looking man, and he had hair most women would be jealous of. He called me into the bathroom one night.

"Baby come here for a minute please," Jerry called to me.

"What? Are we gonna try and squeeze in the shower together? I'm ready!" I said to him.

"Oh yes we are, but first I need a haircut."

"Ok, I'll get the clippers out. Do you want me to just do the sides, or are we going to cut the top a little shorter?" I got the clippers and bent over in front of him. I still knew how to get Jerry's attention.

"We can also just do it tomorrow. Is Brendan in bed?" Jerry was grinning.

"He is, but I think we should get the haircut done tonight," I said as I slowly took my shirt off.

"I'm gonna fill the tub for us, and then we can take showers."

"No, you're not, I thought we were doing a haircut," I said, laughing.

"I know what you're doing," he said while trying to get in between me and the tub. "You know how much I love your body."

"You're right, I do know, and I love it and use it to my advantage. Ok, I'll stop for a few minutes, and let's just get your hair done so we can play without the kids."

"I'm ready to just shave it all off, its fast and easy."

"Really? Are you sure, I don't know," I said.

"Yes, I'm sure. It's too hot for hair anyways," he replied.

I grabbed a pair of scissors and cut all the hair on top very short, and then pulled out the clippers and we shaved his head. Well, let me tell you, I was excited when it was done. Talk about sexy. I was iffy before we cut it, but afterward I told him how turned on I was after the haircut, and he vowed to never let his hair grow again. He washed in the shower and then we took our bath together. Jerry said this new haircut was going to make work easier and he wouldn't need so many hats.

Speaking of work, Jerry's mom and dad would come to stay with us every three months while Jerry was on his cleaning trips. They would watch Brendan every day while I was at work, and they loved being near the beach. They would arrive a day or two before he left and stay a few days after he got back, so we could have time for just us away from the house and not worry about the kids.

It was in 2007 when the business came to a crashing end. We had decided to clean for only one restaurant chain, as they had so many locations. They asked us if we would add more locations to the cleaning schedule. These locations were scattered amongst several states, and some a good distance. We informed them that we could only do the east coast states. Within a few months, we were notified that they a hired a new cleaning company that could service all their locations. We talked with my mother and her husband, cut our losses and the business was no more.

I was still at the electric company and I was paid well, so we had enough money to keep us afloat, but it wasn't enough to do lots of things outside the house with the kids, except for the beach, which was free. We made the best of what we had, and always had fun as a family no matter what we were doing.

Life threw us many curveballs, some sharper than others, but we always got through them. Outside of my day job, Jerry and I spent every moment together. We tried to have other couples come over, but we couldn't seem to make friends with anyone that was fun or who could at least hold a conversation. When people were over, we would get so bored. Once they left, Jerry and I would laugh. We both said that we had more fun alone than with other people.

"Another fun-filled night trying to make friends, can't wait to do that again. I hope we get to have another super boring evening tomorrow. I don't even know why we bother, no one understands our playfulness and desire to have fun, or just talk for that matter. I love all the stares we get." Jerry would rant with sarcasm once our new friends went home.

We gave up on trying so hard to make friends. Jerry and I were sitting outside alone on a quiet evening talking around a backyard campfire.

"You know, I don't understand why you're still with me," Jerry said.

"Oh my God, would you please just stop with that nonsense," I replied.

"Murphy has been by my side all my life, and I warned you about becoming unlucky and you still said, 'I do'."

"You're darn right I said, 'I do' and I would say it again in a heartbeat."

"I love you, baby, you always make me laugh. I will never understand how you always find the light at the end of the tunnel, but it's awesome."

"I have always been that way—you know that—and thank goodness, because someone needs to balance your constant negativity," I said to him, laughing

"Yeah, yeah smart ass. What would I do without you," Jerry replied, shaking his head.

"I'm not sure, but I doubt you'd be as happy, or as angry sometimes. I know I do a good job pissing you off. I don't know what I'd do without you either. Life isn't always sunshine, and rainbows, and I learned that from you," I said as I leaned in for a kiss.

"I don't know what we're gonna do financially, this is getting hard," Jerry said while putting out our fire.

"Just stop worrying, we'll figure it out, we always do," I said. I grabbed his hand and lead him into the house.

"Sarah, I love you! I hope you know that."

"I do, and you know that I am crazy in love with you. Why don't we go play in our room?"

"Baby, you are fucking crazy! Not a care in the world right now, you're amazing," he said.

As we get older

A Soulmates Twin Flame

Jerry's Canvas

Love is Patient

One morning Jerry and I got up early while his parents were staying with us for a visit. We watched a sunrise over the ocean and went pier fishing. I had a great time and we caught many small fish called spot. We had a cooler that our bait was in and decided to save the fish as bait and come back that night. After dinner, we went back to the pier and cut the fish into smaller pieces. I baited my hook and cast my pole into the open waters of the ocean, as did Jerry.

We were talking, laughing and people-watching while still holding onto our poles. I felt a good tug on my pole and began to reel in. I was struggling and asked Jerry for help. This was a strong fish and for a second, I thought I was going to lose my pole in the water. With his help, we reeled the fish in, and our mouths both dropped open when we saw what was at the end of my pole.

We caught a baby shark. I have never been that close to a shark before unless there was glass between us. I asked Jerry to handle that one. I was a little too scared to take the shark off the end of my pole. After a few minutes, he managed to carefully take him off and put him back in the water. Our shark got plenty of attention that night. We couldn't wait to get home and tell the kids.

Jerry and Brendan had become close as he had been home with daddy every day for a little while. Jerry had been trying to teach his son everything he could, and for the most part was a great teacher. I tried to show Brendan how to tie his shoes one day, and that didn't go well. Teaching was an area where I lacked patience. Jerry, on the other hand, only had patience when he was teaching something. He taught Brendan a few things that might not have been appropriate.

"Hi baby, I know I don't usually call you at work, but are you busy?" Jerry asked.

"I know you don't usually call me at work, no matter how many times I tell you it's ok. What happened?"

"Ah, yeah, how do I say this. Can you just take an early lunch and come home, please?"

"Jerry, what's wrong, are you guys ok?" I asked.

"We're both fine, I just need your help with something and kind of quickly, please."

"What is it?"

"Can you please just come home?" He asked again. I was now hearing his impatient, irritated tone.

"Fine, I'll be there in ten minutes. Love you."

I got to the house, walked in the door and saw both my boys sitting on the couch. Jerry was holding a towel on his leg and I could see blood coming through. I asked what happened and before Jerry could open his mouth Brendan jumped up as he was so excited to tell me about his day.

"Mommy, mommy! Daddy is so fun, we had so much fun. Me and daddy played new games today. I was having fun, mommy, and then daddy broke it," Brendan said while smiling and spinning around the room.

"Excuse me, broke what, and what new games is he talking about, honey?" I asked.

"Can you please help me here, there a piece of glass stuck in my leg and I couldn't pull it out."

I lead Jerry into the bathroom and looked at his leg. The piece of glass was thin and small, it was a shard of glass. I didn't ask him, but I think he was scared that it might bleed too much if he pulled it out himself, and he didn't want to see that. I pulled the shard out of his calf and cleaned it, then put a band-aid on it. My big baby was fine and would have been fine without me that day, but never the less I enjoyed helping him and got plenty of affection.

Jerry then told me that he was just playing with Brendan that morning. He was showing him about juggling and decided to try it with a few small plates. One dropped and shattered, and a piece ended up stuck in his calf. I went back to work and finished my day with a smile. When I got home that evening, Jerry and I talked because Brendan was only a year away from starting kindergarten and we both thought that interaction with other children besides his sister would be good for him.

We found a church that offered a preschool program. It was only three hours a day, which was good for both of my boys. Jerry had done everything with Brendan and now it was time for them to separate. Jerry told me one day that he thought Brendan needed constant attention.

"Let him play by himself in his room. He needs to learn to entertain himself," I told Jerry.

Jerry said that he didn't want to miss any moments with his son. He missed so much with his daughter that he didn't want that to happen again. I had noticed that my two boys were attached at the hip. But what would Jerry do while Brendan was in pre-school? My husband had lots of problems not being the breadwinner of the family.

Jerry used his alone time while Brendan was at school to get back into his art. He quit on his artistic abilities when he joined the military but saved all his work. He found a sense of satisfaction in his art, and ever since the first time I saw his old drawings, I thought he was extremely talented. Jerry was also beginning to get frustrated on an almost daily basis as he needs to stay busy and try not to let his mind get the best of him. Jerry said to me one day,

"Sarah, you don't understand. I am trying, this is very hard every day not being the one to go out and support this family. It has been drilled into me since a child that the man needs to always work and support the family. I know I don't need to be the only financial person in the family, but I do need to feel like I am at least contributing, and we are doing this together."

"I understand, but you are contributing and helping. We are getting by financially and do you know how hard it would be to keep my job if I had to worry about the kids and take them to their appointments or pick them up from school. Does it really matter who makes the money? it's about us as one. We are a team, you always say that," I said.

"I know baby, but I can't just sit home, take care of kids and the house even if we are ok financially. I need to help with money, that's who I am. Also, just being home and never leaving, the walls are closing in no matter what I do, I need to get out and we can't afford for me to go and do anything. It's a no-win situation. I need to work and then I won't get so frustrated with everything when I am home. I am gonna keep going with my art while I look for a job."

Jerry got into his art more and more every day while looking for a job. We also agreed that if Jerry worked full time, we would have to look into who would be the one to put their job in jeopardy with everything that we needed to do with the kids.

A few more weeks went by; Jerry was still looking for a job and becoming more creative with his art, but he had periods where he wouldn't do anything all day except stare at the ceiling. I would come home at lunch and for the entire hour, he'd stare at a wall and not move. There were days that not a word was said between the two of us while I was home at lunch. "I am going to back to work, be home soon, my love, " I would say as I left. He would stay silent or I would get, "Yup." This happened on a weekend day one time when we were all home. Jerry woke up, made a coffee, and sat at the desk looking out the window. He would respond when I asked if he wanted another coffee, but that was it. I was shocked; he spent the entire day there in silence while me and the kids talked, played outside, and I watched tv for a little while. He looked as though he was in a trance the entire time unless something pissed him off, and we would get snapped at for nothing. The kids were nervous and didn't understand what was wrong with daddy. They tried to stay quiet and would sometimes whisper to me and each other.

"You don't have to whisper on my account, I'm so fucking tired of this bullshit with you and the kids. No one will even fucking try and talk to me. I'm fucking done!" Jerry screamed out.

The kids and I didn't say anything to him because we didn't want to get snapped at. I hated the negative remarks he made. I assumed it was better to leave him alone, and just act like he wasn't there until he snapped out of it. That was the wrong way to look at it when all he wanted was someone to try and talk to him. The kids and I backed away from Jerry for a while because of his temper and anger. He said we didn't talk to him anymore and he felt all alone every day. He explained all this to me one evening while we were lying in bed, and I told him I was not comfortable when he was in those moods. He said he didn't understand why some days the depression would hit so hard, and he felt lost. Jerry was so mad about money and not contributing. I looked at it as us, he did not. I would say "Hey, honey, we get paid today." And he would respond back, "No, you got paid today, not me."

"It's not me, it's we! What part of we do you not fucking understand! Jerry, it doesn't matter whose name is listed on the check, we are one and do everything together. I wish I could be the one to stay home, and you went to work all day. I have the patience to stay here all day, you don't! There is nothing I can do unless you find the great paying job with all the benefits. Until then you need to get it in your head that it's WE, not ME."

Jerry and I talked more about his boredom and frustrations with being home and his beliefs about needing to contribute financially. We also discussed how talented he was, and he needed to focus on his art more. Every night when it was bedtime, he was smiling, and we still always went to bed together and had fun regardless of what happened during the day. I needed him, and he needed me. We found a way to bring out the happiness when we were alone together.

Regardless of finances, we still tried to do fun things away from the house with the kids periodically. We both said that it was good for us and we needed as a family to get out and have fun, even if that meant spending money we didn't have and paying a bill late or playing the catch-up game afterward. There were many outings that didn't cost a fortune. We would drive to Myrtle Beach and, along the side of the road, there were kiddie parks that were free to enter, and just pay per-ride. The kids loved it. We played mini golf a few times as those are everywhere.

One thing we did as a family that we all enjoyed was strawberry picking. We had more laughter between the four of us doing that than we did many other things. When we picked strawberries we each had a bucket, and Jerry or I would help Brendan. He kept us laughing.

"Mommy, daddy look it. I found a big one. Is this a good one to pick?" Brendan asked.

"Yes, buddy, that one looks great. See how red it is and it's not mushy and doesn't have any bugs or holes on it," Jerry replied.

"Okay," he said. He picked the strawberry and ate it.

That went on multiple times. After a half hour of picking strawberries, Brendan was covered in berries and said he was full and couldn't eat anymore. The three of us were hysterical; his little red face was priceless. We asked to see how many he had in his bucket and he said,

"Look, I found two really big strawberries and I saved them. I did good!"

A Soulmates Twin Flame

For as much as Jerry said he loved my easy going personality, it annoyed him too. It was the Fourth of July; Jerry and I were discussing where to go for fireworks after dinner that evening.

"Hey, baby where do you want to go for fireworks tonight?" Jerry asked.

"I'm not sure, where do you want to go?" I replied.

"It doesn't matter, but there are some places that will take a long time to get home from because of the traffic," he said.

"I don't really care about the traffic and what time we get home. Remember, I'm off of work tomorrow, so it doesn't matter to me where we go."

"It doesn't matter to me either, I'll drive anywhere. you know that."

"Okay, where would you prefer to go? Any ideas?" I asked.

"No ideas, I just want you to be happy. You know I'm up for anything," Jerry said.

"You pick, I'm ok with any place. I'd prefer not a lot of traffic, but it really doesn't matter."

"Ok, then what would be the best place in your opinion tonight," Jerry asked.

"I don't know, it doesn't matter."

"I thought you just said you didn't want to deal with traffic, you must have some idea where you want to go, or at least where you don't want to go."

"No, not really, I don't know, it doesn't matter. As long as I am with you, I'm happy. You decide. You're the one who doesn't know how to put on smile unless you're happy with where we are going."

A few more times of back and forth and Jerry got very irritated. By the time we pulled into the driveway, he was mad. He got out of the car, slammed the door and went into the house.

"What's your problem?" I asked.

"Are you fucking serious right now? Leave me the fuck alone!" *What the hell?* I could see the vein throbbing in his forehead.

"Don't walk away from me, I was talking to you," I said, trailing behind him.

"Do you not fucking understand English anymore! I said leave me alone."

"No, I don't understand what pissed you off."

"Sarah, everything with you is 'I don't know,' or 'It doesn't matter.' I need to know what *Sarah* wants to do. I want you to express yourself more and maybe try and come up with something or at least have an opinion once in a while." He was still angry, but at least he wasn't yelling any longer

"Jerry, I'm sorry. You just don't understand that I am truly happy with anything no matter what it is, as long as we are doing it together. I know you get frustrated at me for that, but that's who I am: The happy-go-lucky, always optimistic girl you fell in love with. Remember all the times you get frustrated because you don't understand how, even at the worst of times or situations, I always find the bright spot. You stop and smile after and say thank you because you love that about me. Yes, I know there is a shitty side to being me too, because I don't always have an opinion. I can find fun in anything when you're with me."

"I know, it just gets irritating always being the one to try and come up with places to go or things to do, and I'm fucking sick and tired of it."

"I know, but the last time I came up with something, you did it, but were miserable the whole time, the rest of us couldn't wait to get home and away from you. I don't understand why you agree to do stuff if you don't want to. Your misery brings all of us down. I will try and come up with things, but don't agree to it just because it was something I thought of. It needs to be something you're going to enjoy too. Why don't we go to Wilmington tonight for fireworks, but you're driving."

There was silence for about two minutes. I was about to go back into the house, and then he opened his mouth again.

"Holy shit, did Sarah make a decision? I am so proud of you honey!" Jerry was laughing now. Not quite sure how I did it, but I was able to turn the anger switch off, even faster than I turned it on.

"Yeah, yeah, keep laughing, we both like our bedtime fun, but there's a first time for everything and I might just get tired tonight, you never know," I gave him a sexy grin.

"Ok, honey, whatever you say. You tired? Yeah right. I love you, baby, always making me laugh, even when you piss me off, and you have gotten really good at that."

"See, I told you. Ten minutes ago, you were so pissed and now we're both laughing. It's that happy-go-lucky in me that you love, and don't try and deny it, and I love you too! Who else would deal with your pissy negative ass every day," I said, smiling.

Bottom line was, Jerry had a lot of free time on his hands, and it seemed to lead to anger and depression, but he refused to see a doctor for what he thought was just boredom. Eventually, his attention and his energy shifted to his artwork. Through the years, he had produced some great pen and pencil sketches, but he got interested in tattoos. I thought this new interest was worth investigating for the sake of Jerry's mental health, so we bought everything he needed to begin practicing tattooing. He spent time learning his equipment and cleaning it. He practiced on tattoo skins and then himself. After a few weeks, I became Jerry's canvas to practice on. I knew his abilities, so I had no doubts that his art would be beautiful. I went against what I swore to myself when I was younger: Never get someone's name or initials tattooed on your body. I no longer felt that rule applied. Jerry was the love of my life and I was not about to say no to beautiful artwork on my body.

Family Time

Celebration of Love

    Jerry and I loved celebrating holidays with the kids and making everything fun and exciting for them. Jerry was really into Halloween. Every year he would go all out with decorations and loved carving pumpkins with the kids. Isabelle was a little confused and excited when we got her ready for trick-or-treating after we moved to the south. She pranced around going door to door showing off her costume, as she didn't have her winter coat, ski pants and boots on, that she was accustomed to wearing over her costume. Jerry enjoyed dressing up, pretending to be a decoration and scare kids while they took candy from his bowl.

    In 2008 jerry and I dressed up and went to an adult Halloween costume contest in Myrtle Beach, South Carolina. Jerry really wanted to try and go all out for this event because first place won five thousand dollars. I was all painted and dressed up as a witch. I know pretty traditional, but then there was my other half. Jerry was dressed as my servant, well not actually sure what you would call him, but servant works. His costume was good. He had a chef coat with blood all over it, his face was scarred and bloody, and he had a chain around his neck attached to a wagon that I pulled around. In the wagon, we had fake body parts and blood and we put dry ice in the wagon to constantly have smoke around us. We didn't win but got many compliments and stares.

Happy Halloween

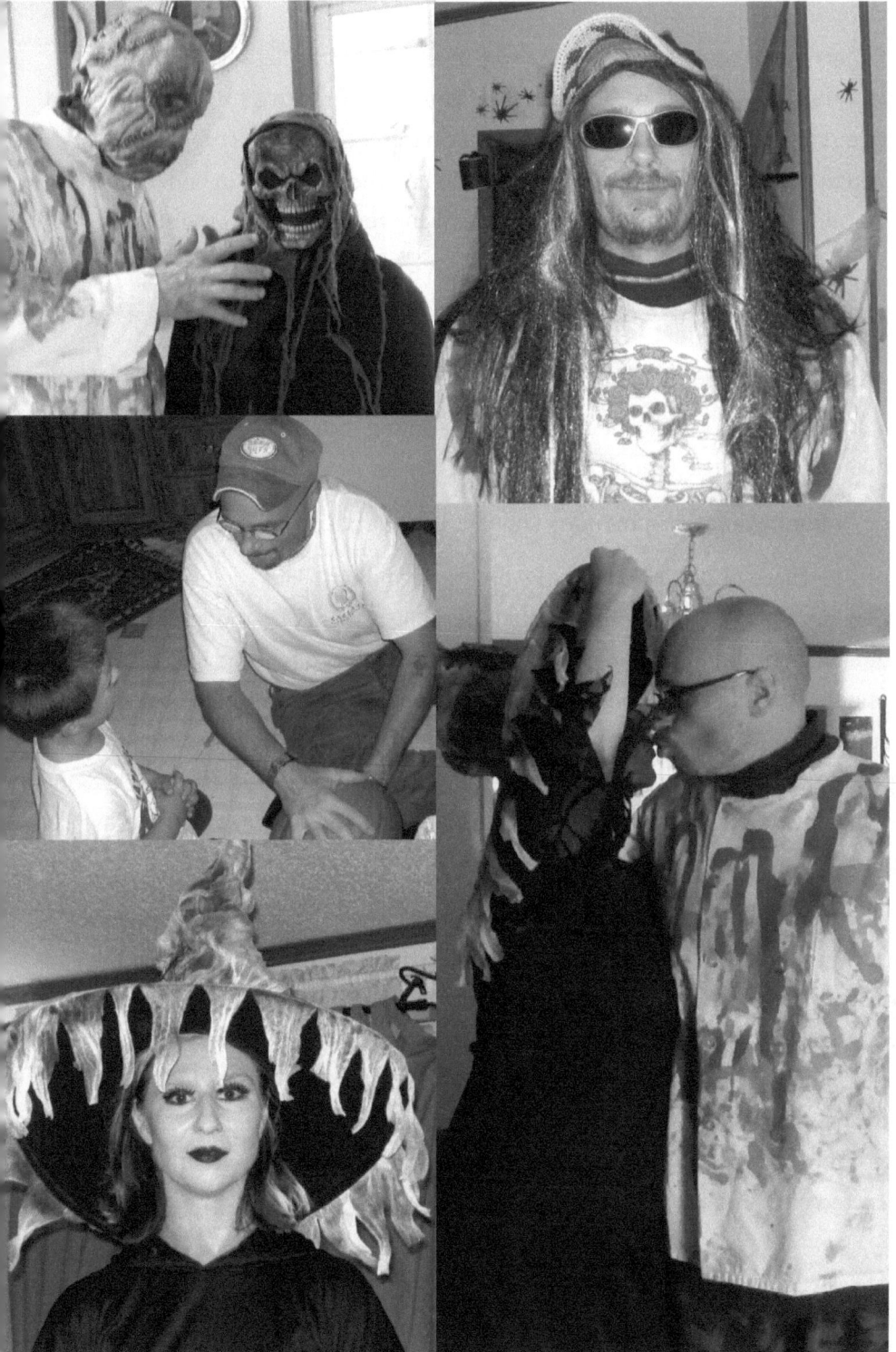

Jerry and I also like playing the role of Mr. and Mrs. Claus. On Christmas Eve Jerry rigged up this contraption. He filled a bucket with a ton of marbles and tied a string to it. He mounted the bucket on the roof and the string came through our bedroom window. That night when the kids were in bed, I got them up, and when Jerry heard us talking in the living room he pulled the string.

"Isabelle, Brendan get up quick, I think I hear Santa and his reindeer on the roof," I said to the kids while waking them up.

"Isabelle, c'mon hurry up, it's Santa," Brendan yelled to his sister all excited

"Okay, listen I think I heard something on the roof," I said as we were walking into the living room.

"Mommy, mommy, mommy I hear it. Let's get daddy!" Brendan said.

The three of us walked into the bedroom and both kids ran over to daddy, woke him up and told him that Santa is here. Jerry, acting as though he was sleeping went out into the living room with us. We both told the kids to go back to sleep, so Santa could come and bring presents and tucked them back into bed. Jerry and I went back and laid down in bed with big smiles knowing that his contraption worked, and the kids were now even more excited. We checked on them a few times to make sure they were sleeping and then put all the presents under the tree.

After that Christmas was over, Jerry finally realized why we had medical insurance and had the ACL in his knee repaired. He said he couldn't take the pain any longer. Wow, that was a long day. The procedure was done, and we were back home the same day. Before we were sent home, Jerry was given a pain pump. A tube was inserted to his knee and the bag was attached to his waist with a clip. We were told to remove it that night before bed. This is when it got fun! Jerry was having nothing to do with removing a tube that was inserted into his body.

A Soulmates Twin Flame

"Alright baby, are you ready? We have to remove the pain pump now," I said.

"No, do we have to. I think there's still medicine in the bag. We can just wait until tomorrow," he replied while having this look of despair in his eyes.

"No, we were told to remove it tonight and you know that if we wait until tomorrow you're just gonna give me the same response again. We are doing this now."

"Whatever dear, but don't expect me to help and please don't tell me about while you're doing it, that's so gross."

Jerry laid down and got into a comfortable position, while I washed my hands and prepared to go to work on my baby. I couldn't help but talk as I was pulling out the tube.

"Holy shit, Jerry this is crazy. I have already pulled out a foot of medical tubing and there's still more. Wow, you can see the blood and pieces of tissue as I pull," I said.

"Okay, please stop, I can't take it, and I think I can feel it now as you pull. I think I'm going to be sick," Jerry said as he glanced over his shoulder to look at his leg.

"Don't look, what are you doing?" I said as he then quickly turned away.

It was a good thing he looked away quickly. I could see in his eyes that he was close to passing out. I thought I might have to slap him like the time I did when we went to Six Flags. We finished, I covered that spot and then wrapped the whole area, so he could shower. I took the next few days off of work to help him.

We have spent many days on the beach over the years and it had lost its luster. Every time we went to the beach we'd come home sticky and covered in sand, and it got everywhere. Brendan still enjoyed playing and swimming at the beach and Jerry would build sandcastles with him. I, on the other hand, tried not to touch anything, except my camera. Jerry and I were both getting back into photography more often. We enjoyed the beach for taking pictures. Watching the way, the pinks and purples would change to tones of orange as the blue started to become dark during the sunsets on the water was beautiful. Some nights we would each have our own camera. Jerry still thought his thirty five millimeter camera was the best and nothing compared. I had a new digital camera.

Our favorite time at the beach was during storms. We could see so far out, and we'd both take pictures. Jerry would say every time that mother nature is fascinating, and nothing compares to what she can create. We spent an hour taking photos one night on the beach when an approaching storm was getting closer.

"Sarah, look over here quick. You see how fast that grey blends with the white, and you can faintly see the rotation of the clouds. Oh, shit, this is awesome," Jerry said

"I see it, I got a few good shots too," I said

"Okay, but so far every time I turned around to look at you, the camera was aimed at me," Jerry replied sarcastically.

"Yes, I got a few of you too. I wanted a few pictures of my sexy man."

"Oh, was your sexy man walking the beach tonight?"

"As a matter of fact, he was." I said.

"Baby look! See how the waves separate. You can see how the land builds up under the water by the way the waves come in. You should get some pictures of the waves too. You know we don't normally see them this big. I would love to have a surfboard right now," Jerry said.

A Soulmates Twin Flame

"How fucking cool would it be if we were storm chasers for the weather channel? You know it would be a fight between us and that other guy, you know who, I forget his name, the one who is at the biggest and worst storms. They say if you see him in your neighborhood, then you better leave, because something wicked is coming from mother nature," Jerry said.

"I know who you are talking about. Darn, right it would be a fight. Imagine having one of those vehicles with all the cool equipment and driving right next to a tornado? That would be fun."

"That will be us one day baby when the kids are grown and on their own. It will be just us doing our adventures again."

"I know, and then we can visit the kids and show them that were not too old to have fun. They already say we're too old. Are you almost ready to get going? I want a smoke and that isn't happening here with this wind," I said.

"Yeah. Let's go, I want one too."

Beach Adventures

A Soulmates Twin Flame

Memorial Day weekend in 2009 we planned a road trip with the kids to visit family in New England. That was a long ride with the four of us packed into a small PT Cruiser and holiday traffic. We finally arrived and went right to my brother's house where we were staying for a few days. My brother had a finished basement with plenty of room and a bathroom. The stairs going into the basement were very narrow. That night as Brendan and I were walking down the stairs, I was looking at him making sure he was holding on to the railing, as I walked down leaning against the wall on the other side. I forgot that the wall ended halfway down. When the wall ended, I immediately fell backward and landed on the floor. Jerry ran over to me and tried to help me up.

"Sarah are you ok?" He yelled as he was running towards me.

"I think so, I hurt, but I'm ok," I replied.

"Give me your hand and we will go sit on the couch together."

"Give me a minute please, it hurts."

"Are you sure you're ok?"

"Yes, I'm fine."

"Baby, I don't mean to laugh but knowing that you are ok, it was kind of funny. I have seen many people fall down the stairs, but certainly not in the fashion that you did," Jerry said while laughing with Brendan.

"I guess it was funny because once again I didn't pay attention. I knew the wall came to end, and I simply forgot. You guys can keep laughing, Ha! Ha!"

I stayed on the floor for a few more minutes until the throbbing stopped in my body and then stood up. In an instant, I fell back down. I didn't feel any pain in my left foot until I stood up. That was so excruciating that it dropped me back to the floor. Jerry again ran back over to me and this time he picked me up and carried me to the couch. He asked me many questions and looked at my foot, and said it sounded like it was broken. I was pissed and said there is no way it's broken and I'm sure it will be fine in the morning. Morning arrived, and nothing had changed. Jerry took me to the hospital, confirmed it was broken, put a cast on my foot that went halfway up my leg, and then we left to go see his mom.

"Jerry, this sucks! I'm sorry. I was so excited about going to Six Flags just the two of us, then this shit happens," I said.

"It's ok, we can still have a good weekend. Don't get me wrong I'm disappointed, but did you really think we were going take a mini vacation and have everything go as planned. Honey, I knew something was going to put a damper on our trip, I just didn't think it would be you," he said while again laughing me.

"I'll let you keep going on with the jokes because you're also going to keep on carrying me around everywhere. I can try the crutches again, but being the klutz that I am, I could end up breaking the other foot," I said while laughing with him.

"I'm gonna stop and run into this store and buy you a few pairs of shorts, so I can get my pajama shorts back. I'll be right out."

"Okay, I think I will just wait for you in the car."

I didn't have any pants or shorts that would fit over the cast, so I borrowed Jerry's. I'm just glad he thought about my clothing situation before they put the cast on. I was wearing Jeans, and those were not coming off unless I cut them once the cast was on. He helped me change before we went to the doctor that morning. Our weekend turned out ok, and we still had fun. Jerry was very tired from carrying me or helping me hop around. He got a break on our last day. My brother had a cookout in his backyard and invited all the family over. He set everything up, so I didn't have to move. It was much easier for everyone to ask me if I needed something while I stayed in a chair all day. Once we made it back home, I called in sick to work for a few days and finally learned how to use the crutches with Jerry's help. I still had another four weeks before I could step on

A Soulmates Twin Flame

that foot. We laughed a lot at the whole situation and Jerry said he was surprised that 'Murphy' was my friend that weekend and not his.

Family fun outings

A Whole Lotta Love

Families that play together stay together

By the time summer arrived, things were looking up: I was back walking again without any help, and Jerry got a new job. He was hired as the chef at a failing restaurant and rose to the challenge of bringing it back to life. I had no doubts in his abilities to do so. I have seen him turn a restaurant around before and bring in a lot of business. We weren't as tight on money, so we celebrated by taking the kids to a new amusement park in Myrtle Beach.

The park was called 'Freestyle Music Park'. Jerry and I went to this park the previous year, just the two of us, when it opened as the 'Hard Rock Park'. I took Brendan on many of the kiddie rides that day, and Jerry went on the small roller coasters with Isabelle. Jerry and I loved the biggest one they had, the Led Zeppelin ride. We rode it so many times, we were both worn out on the song 'Whole Lotta Love'. A trip to the amusement park was the perfect way to celebrate Jerry's new job. The kids had fun, but I would have to say Jerry had the most fun. His facial expressions, captured in photos from that day, were priceless.

Over the next few months, we spent most of our free time at home, usually outside, often around a campfire. Jerry's mom had moved to North Carolina and was living with us while she looked for a place. This worked out well because she was there to take care of the kids until I got home. There were a few evenings the kids and I would walk to Jerry's restaurant for a free dinner. Two incomes were better than one, and we all enjoyed less stress about how bills would get paid.

By December, life had slipped back to what was "normal" for our family. Even though the restaurant was back on track with steady business, he was losing kitchen staff because their paychecks bounced. The electric company had threatened to shut the power off because the bill hadn't been paid in months, and the food vendor demanded payment in advance of delivery. Jerry quit in frustration, and the restaurant closed a few weeks later.

Freestyle Music Park Myrtle Beach

Sarah J Provost

We were back to struggling, and Jerry felt horrible, but I told him to stop worrying.

"We'll figure it out; We always do."

A week before Christmas my mother called about a house that was for rent and she knew the owner. We said ok, we'll check it out. Jerry's mom had moved out of our house in November and went back up North.

It was larger and cheaper than the one we were living in. In just a few weeks, we were packed and ready to go. This was one move which would go smoothly, I thought.

When moving day arrived, it was snowing, the first measurable snow we'd seen in the "Sunny South." Once again, Jerry's friend "Murphy" was there to make sure we didn't get complacent. What could we do but laugh? There wasn't a lot of snow, but enough to make moving day suck while Brendan threw snowballs. When we finished our move, the snow had all melted.

As we settled into our new home over the months, Jerry went back to his art with drawing and tattooing. He still battled with dark days of boredom and depression, blaming himself for our financial situation. When Jerry and I would talk, he'd say that his mind was a curse. It's a gift, I would tell him.

"You can give me ten answers to a question in less time than most people would take to come up with one."

He tried to explain to me about all the different voices in his head, but I didn't always understand. Jerry's art had become what I thought was astonishing, and he was continuing to advance in his abilities.

We invested in his art, adding higher quality materials. At night, he would talk to me about shadows and depth. I would stare at him like a deer in headlights because I had no clue what he was talking about. He would add a new tattoo to my body, and I knew before I looked at it that it was beautiful.

Pencil sketches & poster for Brendan

Sarah J Provost

New Experiences

Love is sharing

2011 was a year to do something different, a time to take on new adventures and shake things up, family-style. The four of us went to the air show in Wilmington, North Carolina. Brendan had the most fun. He couldn't believe all the planes he saw flying. The kids enjoyed getting a ride in a monster truck. The tires were twice the size of them. They sat in a military plane and in a military Hummer. Jerry and I laughed many times. As much as Brendan liked the planes, every time he heard one, his hands would fly up to cover his ears. By the end of the day, his arms were tired.

Jerry and I started cleaning beach houses together every Saturday to help boost our income; it was more money than we initially thought. Don't get me wrong, it was more work than we thought too, but it was one day a week. We liked our Saturdays together, just the two of us, even it was cleaning up after tourists. Some houses we would call beach mansions. We would walk through the whole house if it was one we hadn't been in yet. Many times, we'd show each other things we wanted, or would imagine what our dream house would look like.

"Sarah, come check this out. This is what I was telling you about that I wanted for our kitchen," Jerry would say while I was looking around.

"You have to come and look at this bathroom baby, it is bigger than our bedroom," I said as I walked toward the kitchen to get him.

"Oh, shit! Now that is my idea of a shower for two. Get in, let's see how much room we have."

"There is plenty of room. This works perfect for us, see." I bent over and placed my hands against the wall while he was behind me and had his hands around my waist.

"Okay, we need to get to work before we decide to not clean at all. You can't just bend over in front of me like that all the time and pretend."

"Yes, I can, it's fun," I said as I kissed him.

After ten minutes of checking out the house, we would start cleaning. At the end of the day, we were tired, and couldn't wait to spend the night snuggling on the couch with snacks. Our summer Saturdays lasted through the beginning of October.

Winter had arrived, and Brendan decided he wanted to join the Boy Scouts. We thought this was a great idea for him to get out and make some new friends. Jerry took him to the weekly meetings. He would come home afterward and complain at how boring it was. I brought Brendan a few times, and Jerry would then listen to me complain about how boring it was. After a few more months we started going to the meetings together, so we had each other to talk to while the boys did their activities or just played. It was way more fun when we went together. Jerry and I had no problems laughing at the weird things people do. We tried to make a few friends but didn't seem to really click with any of the other parents.

Before we knew it, it was getting close to summer again.

"Jerry, that call was about summer cleaning. She asked if we could work this Saturday. I said sure!"

"Really, that's awesome. I wasn't expecting to hear from them until May," he replied.

"I just hope it's every Saturday from this point on."

"Yeah, me too. I guess we will see. Time to get our shit together. We have to go to the store tomorrow and get all our chemicals."

"Okay, you know we should try doing a cash bucket like we did when we were younger and that will help save for Christmas," I said.

"We can try it, but you know what goes in the bucket stays there until we are ready for Christmas shopping. I'm just happy that I am contributing money to this family," Jerry said.

"Whatever, you just don't get it. It's we, not me. How many times do I have to tell you."

"How many times do I have to tell you that I was raised differently. My mom wasn't the breadwinner, like yours. I understand where you're coming from. I know you love me and it's about us. It's just really hard for me to watch my wife go to work all day while I stay home and work on my art when my wife doesn't even like her job."

"Your job is harder than mine honey, I will tell you that, and you get paid very well, just not with physical money."

"I know, some days my mind gets the best of me and I have to remind myself that it's mind over matter. I don't mind, so it don't matter. That's my motto."

"Jerry, I love you. Let's go out for a smoke and figure out what we need for the weekend."

That was a long summer. We liked our Saturdays, and even sometimes were asked to clean on Sundays.

Brendan was still in the Boy Scouts and Jerry went with him on his first camping trip. Talk about a long weekend for me. I was not by any means thrilled to be alone. The first night I couldn't figure out what to do. Isabelle was with a friend, and everything was so quiet. I didn't like it. I rented a movie, and Jerry and I talked and texted throughout the evening in-between the activities. That night I had a hard time sleeping. I tried his side, my side, the middle. Nothing was working, I just felt like this is wrong, something is missing. Well, duh, of course, I knew what was missing, but that didn't make it any easier, especially knowing I had to do this again for another night. Jerry called me when he got up Saturday morning.

"Hey baby, were you sleeping? I just needed to hear your voice this morning," Jerry said in delight.

"No, I'm awake. I know, early for me to be up without an alarm, but I just couldn't sleep or get comfortable," I replied back.

"Last night sucked. The ground was hard even with the cushions we brought, and it was lonely. I missed my baby! I just wanted to go home, snuggle and make love to my wife."

"I know, I was hoping I would hear you pull in the driveway and tell me you were home and going to drive back in the morning. Wishful thinking, I guess."

"I thought about talking to Brendan later and see if he wanted to sleep in his own bed tonight; I doubt it but you never know."

"How was yesterday and last night? Did you stay around the campfire much longer after I got off the phone with you? Were there a lot of moms there, or just dads?" I asked.

Jerry then told me about a few of the activities that he didn't get to tell me about the day before and said that they were getting ready for some learning activities and that he would call me later. I spent most of the day cleaning, trying to get as much done as possible, so he didn't have to do anything on Monday and could just work on his art. The night finally arrived, and we had periodically texted throughout the day. We spoke a few times and he told me that there was no way Brendan was leaving. He was having a great time. We talked again that night, and I questioned what he did all day. I again asked him about other people being there. He got frustrated with me and said he will call me when they are on their way home in the morning. They got home early Sunday afternoon and we talked about the weekend.

"Hey baby, did you guys have fun?" I said to Jerry as he walked through the door.

"Brendan had a great time, I am exhausted and sore. How was your weekend?" he asked.

"It was lonely, and way too quiet for my liking."

"Baby, I love you, but you pissed me off last night. I just don't understand. I feel like you don't trust me or something."

"I know. Jerry, I trust you completely. I don't understand why I get like that and ask those silly questions. I would have to say maybe jealousy, but even then, I don't know. Sometimes you get frustrated with me because you say I have no imagination, or I don't express myself enough. I just get the feeling that someday, someone is going to come along and tickle your fancy in a way I can't."

"Sarah, I'm proud of you for at least trying to explain. It's a start on opening up. I am so in love with you, I would think you'd realize that by now. I am married to the most beautiful woman I have ever met, with a huge heart. I am not going anywhere, and there will never be anyone that tickles my fancy like you do," he said.

I really didn't understand why I felt the way I did about Jerry finding someone else, or me not being enough for him. I would tell myself how lucky I was that I was his wife. I wanted to scream from the rooftops how in love I was. I had been told over and over that if it seems too good to be true, then it usually is. We had been together for 15 years, and I was still crazy for him. Still, I just couldn't seem to get it through my thick skull that he wasn't going anywhere.

A Soulmates Twin Flame

Jerry had many quirks and was by no means perfect, nor was I, but there was a feeling inside me that said together we were perfect.

Not long after Brendan's first camping excursion, we got a phone call from my mom. She asked Jerry if he would like to bartend at a local bar a few nights a week. Her friend was the owner and was looking for help. Jerry said sure, as it was offseason from summer cleaning and an opportunity to make money. That job lasted a few months and he quit. He didn't get paid very well hourly, and many people didn't tip. His biggest problem was his own fear. Bartending laws differ from state to state. Jerry was uncomfortable serving someone who had already had a few too many. He was accustomed to being held responsible if they left his bar and got in an accident because he served them too much alcohol. You had a right to say I am not serving you, I think you had too many and you're driving. That wasn't the case here. Jerry said he couldn't take it, seeing that many people shitfaced walk to their cars and drive away. He was so frustrated by this that he quit.

When the cooler weather moved in, we started our backyard campfires. Many nights we spent the evening outside around a fire, sometimes with a bottle of wine or coffees, and we'd talk about things we wanted to do or large projects that needed to get done. Some nights Brendan would join us and sometimes even Isabelle, but not as often for her unless the fire was really big. We were all pyros. My favorite time for a backyard fire was after Christmas. I couldn't wait to watch the tree go up in flames, as that was our biggest blaze each year.

Sarah J Provost

Painting the Walls
Letting out the inner child

I arrived home from work one evening and could sense Jerry's frustration. I knew I had to come up with something creative. He needed more than just his pencils and paper. His creative mind was never-ending. It wasn't long after dinner when an idea just popped into my head.

"Jerry, come here for a minute, please. I want to ask you something," I yelled out.

"What is it, baby?"

"I know the landlord said that we could paint the walls or do whatever we wanted if it was going to be an improvement to the house," I said.

"Okay, go on"

"Well, you painted Isabelle's walls purple for her, these walls are so boring just being white, why not paint a mural or something," I said hesitantly.

"I could, and you know what, that might be fun. Maybe I can do something in 3D or create a whole story."

"You could do anything on these walls. You say your art sucks, but I'm sorry, I think it's incredible and I want to see more."

"Baby, you're awesome, but we don't have the type of paint I would need, and all the different colors and brushes would just be more than what we can afford."

"Who cares, let's go to the store tonight and look at some stuff. We're not doing anything else this evening," I said.

A Soulmates Twin Flame

"Okay, let me rephrase that, we can't afford shit. I would love to try and paint, but it's just not gonna happen."

"Would you stop, please. So, we spend a little money and I spend a little more time looking for coupons, and finagling finances. You always said that sometimes we just need to say screw it and have a good time even if it takes a little money. Baby, this is one of those times. I'll figure it out, stop worrying, and put your shoes on. We are going to the store."

We went to the store and bought a bunch of bottles of different color paints and brushes. We went with the cheap paints, as this was just for fun anyways. I told Jerry that I had already figured out about the money, and in fact, I had. Jerry and I paid attention to our electric usage and soon we were saving money. It didn't sound like a lot daily, but at the end of the month, it was a good savings. Don't get me wrong, it was hard in the beginning. I liked having scalding hot water and having to use the cold to make it just right. The energy saving temperature most certainly took away how much cold was needed. We adapted to the energy-saving lifestyle.

By the end of the week, Jerry had finished three-quarters of the room with a 3D China theme. I was in complete awe when I looked at it. The first wall had a bamboo forest with mountains, and as you looked around the room there was the 'Great Wall of China' and a bridge at the corner of two walls that gave you the impression you could walk across it. He also had a dragon on top of a tower and ninjas. I knew Jerry was talented, but I never imagined anything like this. I think what blew me away the most was that he painted everything from his imagination to put the scene together. He didn't use any pictures for reference. To me, Jerry's mind was like a large photo album. He saw something once and he remembered every small detail. I had heard that left handed people are very talented or naturally gifted. I never thought much about it before, but Jerry was left handed. His right hand seemed nonexistent, and he couldn't do anything with it.

Even during that new painting week, he still found time to do everything with the kids, the house was always clean, and we always ate really good. Jerry said you eat with your eyes first, and he wanted to make sure his family ate like that every day. I couldn't figure out he managed of all of it in an eight hour day while I was at work, but he did.

I had not seen Jerry that excited about something in a while. He had the energy level and happiness of a child on Christmas morning. We were both floating on cloud nine. I thought to myself, *could this be it? Is this what he was supposed to do? He has a gift, and we finally figured it out. Maybe this was his calling the whole time, and it just took us a while to make the discovery. He is so happy, we have to keep going with this.* Jerry had told me many times that he enjoyed being a chef, especially when he was given the freedom to get creative with food, but he felt like something was missing, or it just wasn't enough.

"Jerry, I can't believe it. I don't even know what to say, this is amazing, and that's not even enough. The walls are unbelievable. I want you to try something for me. Could you paint me a nighttime ocean theme with a dolphin and a lighthouse?" I asked

"Fuck yeah! Oh my God, Sarah, painting is awesome. You don't even understand how limited I have been with just pencils and paper. I can be me, I can express myself like never before. This is it, I feel it. Are you ready? Let's go to the store and get a few things," Jerry said.

We went to the store that night and bought a few more things. This was the first time in a while that Jerry did not mention anything about money or even ask if we had the money. I didn't say anything to him about either. I told myself that I'd figure it out later. That night I watched him paint for a while. He didn't leave his chair for hours. I saw what started as a brush stroke turn into a dolphin.

A Soulmates Twin Flame

"How did you do that? How did you remember all those small details on the dolphin and the lighthouse?" I asked

"Baby, once you've seen one lighthouse, then you've basically seen them all. I have seen many lighthouses. Remember when we saw that documentary on the dolphins a few years ago? They showed a dolphin many times and some good close-ups," he replied.

"I know, and I remember watching it, but I can't tell you all the little details of the dolphin like you have it painted unless I was looking at a picture or something."

"You know this by now honey, that's just how my mind works. I don't know how else to explain it to you. Why do you think I get so mad sometimes? I can't always control all the voices, and the images are so clear. It's rather frustrating."

"I know, maybe someday I will get it. I need to take a few pictures, and then are you ready to shower with me? I do have to get up for work in the morning."

I went to work the next morning and brought the camera with me. I had to show all the girls Jerry's painting. I went to work glowing, and it was noticeable to many. To the first girl who said something, I whipped out the camera and said, "You are not going to believe this, look at what my husband did!" I showed her the painting and she was in awe. I showed many other people that day and they were all amazed.

This new found passion really seemed to open Jerry's world. The depression and moodiness disappeared, and the creativity flowed out. In addition to his painting, he thought up inventions, and put his ideas on paper. We didn't have the money to execute the ideas, but that didn't stop the flow. At night, we would watch tv together and sometimes see Jerry's inventions advertised.

"See, I told you that would have been a good one. Someone else had my idea, except they had the money to make it," he would say.

Jerry turned half the garage into his art studio and was loving his new job, but then came a day that surprised me.

"Good morning baby!" I said

"What's so fucking good about it?" Jerry replied. How could he wake up miserable when he went to sleep happy? I could never figure that one out, but I kept my thoughts to myself as I made coffee.

I sat down on the couch next to him and there was silence for about ten minutes. We both stared at the tv, but neither of us seemed to be watching it. Should I suffer the silence and wait for Jerry's bad mood to change? That might take the whole day. I reached out and grabbed Jerry's hand. He looked up and moved his hand closer to mine, while our fingers intertwined. His gaze softened.

"I need some more coffee. How about you?" I asked

"Sure, please. Thanks, baby."

The rest of the day was fine, and no one was miserable. Nothing bothered me more than seeing Jerry miserable, or hurt, or whatever he was feeling. I would probably never understand his moods. But most of the time, changing them was as easy as taking his hand, and I could do that.

No more boring white walls

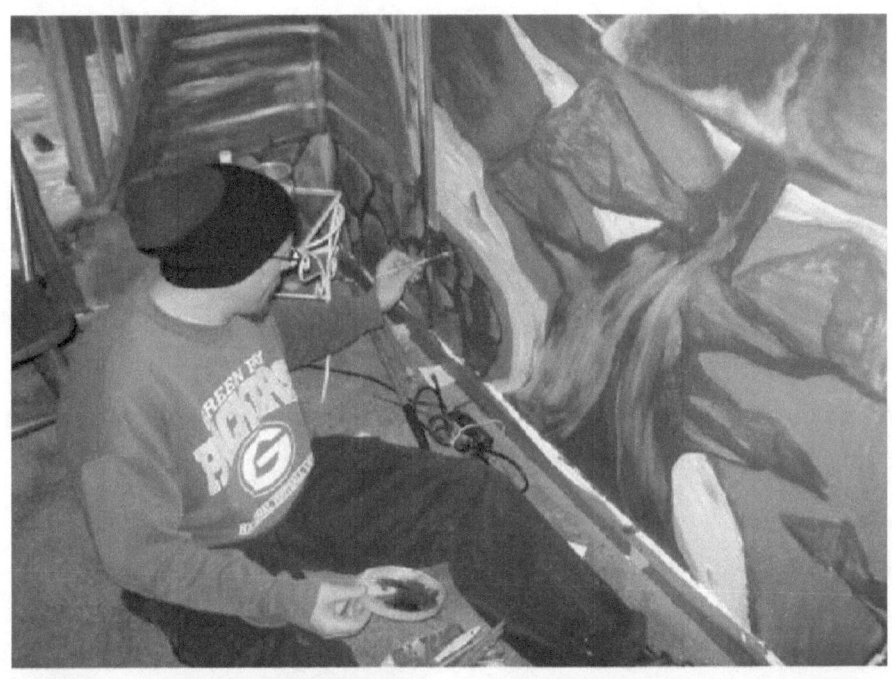

Sarah J Provost

Murphy Spends the Weekend

Love brings laughter

Another Boy Scout camping trip had arrived in Spring 2013. Jerry and I went together with Brendan on this camping trip. We arrived and the three of us checked out everything there was to do. It was already late in the afternoon, so we did our setup, collected firewood, and made dinner.

We sat around a fire talking while Brendan and a few friends played flashlight games. It started to rain right as we were going to get ready to call it a night. Jerry and I sat at the picnic table while Brendan was in the tent. We were laughing while trying to stay dry smoking a cigarette. The rain came down harder, and not long after that, it was pouring. We were soaked. Brendan inside the tent was soaked along with everything we had. Jerry and I didn't bring a rain cover for the tent, didn't think we would need it. We didn't know what to do since the rain was not stopping. We grabbed the important stuff, hopped in the car and drove home. We arrived back early the next morning with dry blankets and towels.

The day after the rainstorm our weather was beautiful, and a bit cold for that time of the year in the south, but we weren't complaining. The three of us cleaned up our mess, got rid of the wet firewood and hung everything up to dry. We enjoyed the rest of the day talking, hunting for dry firewood (unsuccessfully, we went and bought some), and doing activities that were offered. Jerry made dinner again that evening, and we again sat around our little fire.

A Soulmates Twin Flame

"I can't believe how nice it was out today, with yesterday being so hot. I noticed many other campers bringing little heaters into their tents, while you were cooking. Why would they want heaters?" I said.

"I don't know momma, that's weird. Let's take a walk and buy one more thing of firewood," he said.

"See, look more people bringing in heaters. Ok, that's not a good sign," I said while we were walking to the campground store.

"Baby you don't have to worry. These people don't know what real cold is. Its April in the south, how cold do you really think it would get. We have extra blankets if needed."

"I should have checked the weather."

"Honey, you got me to keep you warm, what more do you need?" Jerry said.

"Not a darn thing my love!" I replied.

I was curious about the weather, so I asked someone at the campground store.

"Okay, so I found out that the forecast for tonight is below freezing and record-breaking temperatures," I said.

"Are you fucking kidding me? We don't have enough blankets, and we certainly don't have enough money for a tent heater. Baby, I know what we're going to do," Jerry said with a smile.

"Alright my love, what ideas do you have?"

"Could you please get Brendan, we are going to the store."

"What store, and what do we need?" I asked.

"I saw a liquor store while we were waiting in the McDonalds parking lot earlier."

"Oh yeah, I saw it just didn't think anything about it. I know what you're thinking baby. It's been many years since we stayed up all night drinking. Are you ready for some fun?" I asked.

We bought a bottle of rum, a few bottles of coke, and a few extra packs of smokes to get us through the night. We also got more firewood. Jerry got our fire going and Brendan was too cold and tired to stay up, we got him all set up in the dry tent. He used every single blanket we brought to keep warm. I already knew he was going to need them all when I heard the weather. Jerry and I made cocktails and sat close to the fire all night drinking, laughing and talking about all the other people, and the crazy things we see. I couldn't tell you how many times Jerry said to me, "You need to keep your voice down, Shh! Whisper, baby, whisper." I had to remind him a few times too. It had been years since Jerry and I had drinks. I had a great night. We both were complaining about being tired and finally called it a night at four-thirty in the morning. We squeezed into the corner of the tent and snuggled as close together as possible. Brendan was out cold, and there was a blanket he wasn't using. We wrapped in it, but it wasn't enough. I never fell asleep and shivered for an hour as did Jerry. We got up and sat by the fire again. Once Brendan was awake, we had breakfast, packed our stuff, and went home.

It was by no means our best camping adventure, but my cheeks were sore for a while from all the laughter we shared. I even had Jerry's cheeks hurting that night. That last night in between his hysterical laughter, Jerry said, "Murphy just wanted to spend the weekend with us." It's funny and I laugh, at least most of the time I laugh, but not a day goes by where Jerry and I don't look at each other and say, "Go Figure." It's not normally something major, but it's always something.

It was a beautiful day outside, the sun was shining, it was neither hot nor cold. You couldn't have asked for better weather, and there had been no wind for a few days, not even a slight breeze. The trash needed to go out, so I told

A Soulmates Twin Flame

Jerry I'd be right back. Still, a gorgeous day and I walked towards the trash barrel. As I got close, a huge wind gust came, and the barrel was thrown over by the wind, and trash was everywhere. In an instant, it was over, and back to not even the slightest breeze. This was not a light barrel either and was almost full of trash. I chuckled to myself, and said, "Whatever, gonna take a lot more than that to make me angry, better luck next time!" I was talking to thin air but that's ok. Jerry ran outside when he heard the wind.

"Sarah! Are you ok? What was that noise I just heard?" Jerry asked.

"I'm fine, what you heard was a wind gust and it knocked the barrel over," I said.

"No seriously, what was that noise?"

"I'm telling you it was a wind gust."

"Honey, there's no wind today, not even a breeze. So, you're telling me that a wind gust out of the blue, from nowhere blew over the barrel?"

"Yes, and what you heard was the wind and that branch hitting the roof. I'll be in a minute."

Jerry was hysterical laughing as he went back in the house. When I went back in, he was still laughing.

"Baby, I'm sorry I don't mean to laugh at you, but that shit is too funny," he said.

"Yeah, whatever, keep laughing. I'm glad it wasn't you! That trash was nasty, and I know all I would have heard is you screaming and swearing."

"Your right, I would have been pissed. It's still funny, mostly because it was you. I think 'Murphy' is trying really hard to be your friend too lately."

"I'm kind of thinking the same thing. It still baffles me about the wind, not even a breeze since then."

Sarah J Provost

There was not another wind gust or a breeze all day, nor the next day. Jerry was still laughing the next day about it too. He is always reminding me that I was warned before I said my vows that he was unlucky, and his best friend was 'Murphy'. I told Jerry one day that I am the luckiest woman in the world, and he's the luckiest man. We have each other and two great kids. He didn't see it that way at first, but it didn't take long.

"Sarah, your right. I am the luckiest man in the world. You're with me! I'm so in love with you. I just don't always see things the way you do, but I am learning. I don't think my cup is half empty anymore, but it's certainly not half full either," Jerry said one night while lying in bed.

A Soulmates Twin Flame

Roll with It

Love is unconditional

Jerry and I opened an online Etsy store in 2013 to sell the paintings that were hanging on every wall of our home. While we waited on that venture to take off, we decided to take off as well! It had been some time since our last road trip to New England, and Jerry and I both missed it. We wanted to take another trip with the kids to go apple picking and enjoy Mother Nature's colors. But first we needed a new car.

Jerry and I had spent the last month so frustrated with our old car. It had so many problems. We finally got to a dealer a month before our road trip and looked at many cars.

"My love, we are obviously not getting a new car today," Jerry said to me.

"Oh, yes we are!" I replied.

"He has already said that it will be hard because we owe more than our car is worth, and our credit isn't good."

"I'm sure there is some bank that will help us; give it a few more minutes," I said as the guy was walking back to us.

"See, baby I told you it's not gonna happen. He just said the payment would be over five hundred a month. We can't afford that. Let's just go home and try to work on our credit. We can try again another time. We made it this far and figured out how to do everything together using our old car; a couple more months won't kill us," Jerry said.

"I am not leaving here in that stupid, ugly piece of shit we call a car! I can figure this out," I replied.

"I know you can, but it kills me because you don't ask for help. You get so frustrated with all that calculating you do all the time, and you don't let me in on what's going on or if I can help you. You say we don't have money, but I don't know if that means we can't take the kids out for ice cream or we aren't even going food shopping until the next paycheck. I need to know these things."

"Alright, alright, but no getting mad when you don't understand my finagling or can't figure it out," I said.

The salesman came back again and said the payment would be four hundred and fifty, and he told us about everything included in the loan. There were so many different types of insurances and guarantees. I asked if all that was optional, and he informed us it was, but most people don't get the bare minimum with a loan. I told him to get rid of all the extras and asked what the amount would be after that. He came back, we agreed, signed papers and drove home in our new car. I was so stinking happy that night.

Our trip up north was more spacious, but just as much of a nightmare as the time before. We dealt with so much traffic and issues along the way, that we were all at each other's throats. The last hour of the ride was silent. When we arrived, it took a little while before Jerry and I would even speak to each other. His mouth would get the best of him, and I didn't deserve his frustrations. I ignored him until he apologized. Normally I can't stand the silence. Even if he had been nasty for no reason, I would still walk over, hug him and forget that it ever happened. Not this time. I thought about what Jerry's mom always said to me.

"Sarah, I know how much you love him, but it looks to me like you always put him on a pedestal. You have to stop that. He's not perfect and never will be. He doesn't belong on a pedestal and that's coming from his mother. It's ok to get angry once in a while; it's actually quite healthy."

A Soulmates Twin Flame

I didn't feel like I put him on a pedestal though. It was hard to stay mad at someone I loved so much.

The few days we spent up north were fun. The four of us went apple picking. Brendan said he had a great time. He didn't remember the last time we went, but I did. I had pushed him around the orchards in a stroller the whole time.

Thanksgiving arrived that year and I was glowing with happiness. Jerry did a countdown the two weeks prior because during the holiday seasons I got multiple days off.

"Alright baby, only one more week, then its two days and a wake-up, then you're stuck with me for four days," he said.

We spent the entire holiday in the kitchen, cooking and cleaning as we went. We also played a lot together. There wasn't always conversation, but the silence was companionable as we washed dishes and occasionally splashed one another. Jerry's favorite trick was to tease me with food.

"Oh mama, you got to taste this. You are going to love it," Jerry said.

"Let me grab a spoon," I replied.

"No, you don't need a spoon, I said taste, not shovel it in. You can lick it off my finger."

"C'mon, you know that's not enough for me to actually taste it, I need a spoon."

"No, cause then you double dip, or you just keep sampling everything, and then you're always full before dinner is even served because you ate all day long. I can't trust you in the kitchen alone. Do you want a lick or not?" Jerry was holding the dish just out of reach.

"Please baby, I just want to try it, please."

"Ooh, I like it when you beg. What does daddy get if mama gets to use her spoon?" he asked.

"Daddy knows what he gets," I said. I got on my knees, pulled down his pants and gave him a preview.

"You can use your spoon, and we'll continue that later."

"Oh yeah, I'm gonna continue later."

Jerry knew his kisses sent me to cloud nine, and he totally took advantage. Before dinner was ready, he came up behind me and kissed my neck. Then he turned me around and kissed me some more before turning and walking away.

"Really, you're just gonna walk away. That's not fair," I said.

"What's so fair about what you do to me every single day, anytime you get an opportunity."

"Yeah, so your point? You like it, and so don't I. You know that, and I'm gonna do it again too."

I got down on my knees again and Jerry grabbed me, pulled me back up, and lead me into the bedroom. He kissed me again, then leaned me over the bed. Five sweaty minutes later we cleaned up and went back into the kitchen. Jerry, being the cook, always knew when he had the time to get really playful and take ten minutes from the kitchen, or just tease me. I had no clue about the food part, I was there to sample, clean and play.

We continued with our silly games and teasing each other while finishing dinner and waiting for my mother and her husband to arrive. The food was delicious as always. When dinner was over there were piles of dishes again. I turned on the water, and nothing came out. We checked the bathrooms and no water. We walked into the garage and found out our water pump broke at some point that afternoon. Jerry was a little upset, but not for long because I was hysterically laughing, and he thought it was funny too.

"You know I don't mean to laugh, but it's just too funny. The one day of the year when there are more dishes to wash than any other day and, go-figure, we have no water. It's also funny because there is nothing we can do about it until tomorrow," I said.

"You're right, there's nothing we can do until tomorrow. Get your shoes on, baby, we are going to fill some water bottles."

Jerry and I told the kids we would be back in twenty minutes and went to the county water filling station with all our water bottles and any large bottles we could find and filled them all. Jerry was used to filling water bottles once a week already, as we used city water for drinking and cooking. We didn't like the well water. We filled the sink with soapy water and put as many dishes as we could in there. The larger pans were filled with soapy water and placed outside on the back table until the morning. We had a few gallons for flushing the toilets and saved some for our sponge baths. Nothing was going to put a damper on our evening. When it was time for bed, Jerry and I both got naked, went into the bathroom and gave each other a sponge bath. That was the coldest bath I ever had. We used our space heater to warm up before we jumped into bed together. I had a great night, like most evenings.

The next morning, we called the landlord, told him what happened and that we were going to fix it, and deduct the cost from the rent.

"Alright momma we are going to do this together," Jerry said when we had the new water pump. "You know when you're around me it helps with my patience."

"I know, baby, that's why we do everything together, and because when I'm not around and you fix something, your temper breaks other things in the process," I replied.

"I know, you have told me ten million times already. As crazy as it sounds, I don't get as irritated if I know you're right there, and if I do, you're there to remind me that something silly and stupid is nothing to get pissed over."

"At least you're starting to realize. I love you baby, more than you know! You ready to get to work?"

Jerry and I spent hours installing the new pump. In the process, we also re-did the plumbing to make the water pressure better. We didn't have to, but Jerry thought the setup and all the angles were unnecessary and decreased our pressure. We tested the water when we finished, everything was good, and the pressure was great. We ran into the bathroom and turned on the tub. To our surprise, our plumbing efforts worked out. We had not taken a bath together since we moved into this house. It took so long to fill that, even with the hottest water, it didn't stay hot enough. I was so excited.

"Baby, look how fast the tub is filling. This is awesome!" I said.

"Are you shitting me? It actually worked. Something went right. Wow!"

"Okay, I'm gonna let it fill and see how long it takes," I said.

"You can tell it's not going to take long. Since you're filling it, you might as well take those clothes off and get in," Jerry said.

"Only if you're going to join me."

We both got in the tub. It took a few minutes getting in as it was so hot, but it was awesome. It had been too long since I got to snuggle in the tub with Jerry. After that, Jerry and I never bathed alone. We lit candles and shut the lights off. A few times Jerry put rose petals in the tub. We acted like adolescents, and we loved every minute of our immaturity.

By New Year's Eve, we had lots to celebrate. Jerry had sold his first painting online! In the studio, he had set up a workspace next to his so I could market his painting, monitor the online store and research ways to expose him as an artist. His creativity and my legwork were paying off, and it elevated Jerry's mood to a whole new level. Making art was one thing but selling his art—having other people value his work—had always been just a dream. As we rang in the New Year, I rejoiced in my dream and Jerry's. What more could a girl ask for?

I was also the photographer for Jerry's paintings.

"I'll be right back. I forgot to bring down the camera," I said

I grabbed the camera and a drink for us. When Jerry was happy, he was never afraid to let me know how in love he was. I showed him my love more physically than verbally. Jerry never shied away from the verbal affection.

"Baby look!" I said as I snapped a surprise picture of him when he turned my way.

"Not again. The camera should be aimed at my paintings. If you keep taking pictures of my ugly ass, your camera is gonna break. Don't you have enough already?"

"No, I don't have enough. I like pictures of my sexy husband."

"Baby here put my glasses on, obviously your vision is bad."

"My vision is fine."

"Honey, I love how you always live in a dream world with your sexy husband."

"Yeah, Yeah. I need better lighting for these photos."

Surprise as we get older

More photo fun

Sarah J Provost

Sex and Drugs

Love is never lonely

As a couple and as a family, we had become isolated, in our own little world. Our lack of friends never bothered me. In fact, I didn't even notice it until my sister threw it in my face.

"It's not healthy to have just Jerry. You guys need other people in your life, and besides, it's gross. Don't you get tired of him? I know I would," she said.

"I don't get tired of him. I'm the first one out the door at work because I can't wait to see him. What's wrong with that? We love each other, and have fun together," I said.

"Oh, you are so fucking gross. I don't know how you can stand being with him. He's annoying."

"That's your opinion. I love him. I feel sorry for you that you haven't found someone who you really love and can never get enough of. It's an amazing feeling," I replied.

"Well, it sure wouldn't be someone like *him*, I can tell you that!"

"I have to go, I'll talk to you later."

I was irritated with my sister. I didn't like how she talked about my husband, and I felt sorry for her. She had never experienced a love like that, so why was that my problem? As long as we were happy together as a family, it was nobody's business if we shared that with outside friends or not. As the years flew by, my desires to run to him, to be by his side got stronger, not weaker.

A Soulmates Twin Flame

Jerry seemed to share my feelings. He would tell me that my lunch hour with him was the best part of his day until I got home at five. Some days during lunch he would show me what he was working on, or we'd talk and there were many days where we played. Here's an exchange on an average lunch hour:

"What are you doing?" Jerry asked. He was sitting beside me on the couch.

"Enjoying my lunch hour with you," I said, running my hands between his thighs.

"You might not want to start that right now, or you're going to be late going back to work."

"I won't be late, you don't worry about that," I said. I unzipped his pants and kissed every exposed area.

"Oh yeah, you're gonna be late today," he said.

"Nope, you just sit back and let me have my fun, please."

A few minutes went by and Jerry started talking again.

"Wow, I mean, wow! Baby, you are incredible. You need to write a book or something and let other women know how you do it. Every time is just fucking incredible!"

"It's not something I can share. Without the love, it would be just a boring blowjob, and it would feel more like a chore. I enjoy kissing every inch of you and letting my tongue explore."

"Baby, I do understand. You know I'm no different when it comes to your body. Your curves drive me crazy! I just wish other people knew that even after fifteen years it still feels like those first few weeks together. Sometimes all you do is walk in the room with that silly smile, and I can't take it."

"You're funny. I do have to get back to work now, or I will be late." I gave him a kiss, told him I loved him and left.

Sarah J Provost

My attraction to Jerry was like a magnet to metal. I could never get enough. I still felt butterflies in my stomach when Jerry kissed me after fifteen years. I knew he had the same physical attraction towards me. The way he looked at me and touched me. He couldn't keep his hands to himself either.

I got a surprise one day when I got home from work.

"Momma, I want to show you something," Jerry said as he led me into the garage.

"Oh my God! A new bed frame! Is it finished?" I asked.

"Yes, it is. They just don't make things the way they used to," he said, sounding like somebody's grandpa. "Everything now is so cheap because they want you to spend money and keep buying new shit. Well, we can't afford new shit all the time, so I made us a frame that will last."

"I can't wait to test it and have our mattress off the floor. We'll know by the end of the night how good a job you did."

We brought the frame into the bedroom, and wow was it heavy. It got a good work out that night, and never again did we hit the floor with a thud.

In addition to our love, another of Jerry's pleasures was smoking marijuana which he had smoked every day since long before I ever met him. He said that it helped to calm his mind, and as he got older, it helped with his pain. In fact, it was such a constant, that I only noticed a change in his personality when he wasn't smoking. Without smoking he would become irritated, and his fuse was the shortest I had ever seen. One day his mom said she had never seen Jerry when he was high. I explained to her that she had never seen him *not* high.

"Mom, my baby smokes throughout the day, every day and has since the day I met him." It was true. Marijuana to Jerry was like Advil to someone else.

One evening Jerry headed out to pick up some marijuana while I waited at home. He was only to be gone ten minutes. I made us a pot of coffee, got the laundry going and then sat on the couch, watching T.V. Out of the blue I had an awful feeling in my stomach and felt like I was going to be sick. *Somethings wrong, somethings wrong, where's my baby?* I walked outside smoked a cigarette, went inside to see what time it was, and back outside to smoke another cigarette. I wasn't sure what time he left, but it felt like it had been a while. I called his phone and no answer, it was ten seconds later that he pulled into the driveway.

"Yes, my love, I'm ok. I was thinking of you when I got pulled over. I had a feeling you'd know, or at least feel something wasn't right," Jerry said. He got out of the car, and I threw my arms around him.

"What happened? I was so scared."

"So, after I got my bag, I was driving home, and a cop pulled me over. He said I didn't make a complete stop at the stop sign. Two other cops got out and they asked me to step out so they could search the car and asked if I had any drugs. I thought my best bet was to be honest and listen. I thought about you and stayed calm. I didn't get mad. I gave them the bag and said that was all I had. They thanked me for being honest and obviously, they didn't find anything in the car. I think they appreciated the cooperation, because they were nice after that, gave me a ticket with a court date and let me go home. I wish they would have given me my bag back. I bet they're gonna smoke it, those assholes."

"I am just so happy you are home. What about your bag? You still don't have anything. Can you call your guy back and maybe we can get one tomorrow? We're not going back out tonight," I said.

"Yeah, I'll call tomorrow. I need something," he said.

I was not happy that Jerry was unable to get bag that night. When he wasn't high, he had a short fuse and was irritable. I didn't like it. It was like he had no sense of humor when he wasn't smoking.

Jerry and I had argued over the years about his short fuse and temper a few times. We also argued about me having too long of a fuse and letting the kids walk all over their mother.

"Sarah, I just can't take it anymore. I don't think I can live like this. It eats me up inside and drives me insane when I watch the way the kids have no respect for you. You never say anything, and then I have to be the bad guy every time. I was raised differently. You support this entire family, and they show you no appreciation. I can't watch it anymore, I just can't. It's like nails on a chalkboard for me and it's been going on for years. We have talked about this too many times, and you just let it go in one ear and out the other. I'm done, I have had enough. I just don't think this is going to work. You don't seem to understand how much it hurts me to see that." Jerry said.

"I watch the way you fly off the handle over nothing and I have watched the kids run and hide just wondering if they did something wrong. It breaks my heart to think that they are scared when they didn't do anything wrong. You scream and get so angry and carry on at something as simple as a fly getting into the house because a child was not fast enough to shut the door. That eats me up. I'm sorry I don't know how to get angry, but you get angry enough for the both of us, and I have had enough," I said.

"Sarah, I love you, that's why it bothers me so much, but I just don't know if I can take it."

"I will try to pay more attention and say something to the kids when I feel they are disrespectful. I don't always see it. Tell me when you think it's disrespectful and why, then I will talk to them myself. You don't need to always be the bad guy, but I just don't notice it. Jerry, we need to help each other, like we always have with everything, and I will try my best to help you with the anger, but that's not easy either. Sometimes I just want to hide because I don't like listening to you, nor do the kids."

A Soulmates Twin Flame

"Sarah, I do love you, but again, you know how I feel. We've had this same conversation before, and within a week you forget, and there are the kids walking all over you and you don't even notice. I want to try again, I really do, but this is the last time."

Jerry and I had also laughed many times about our balancing effect and how we complement each other, days after we would have one of our arguments. I'd love to say the conversations about me never getting mad at anything and him blowing his top at nothing only happened once, but no that happened a couple of times. After a while, we finally got it through our thick skulls and actually listened to what the other had to say.

"You know what, momma, I can't help but laugh sometimes. You are an amazing woman to put up with someone like me, and you're still here. I'm not sure why you haven't left me yet. I know you say you're lucky, but I'm beginning to believe that I'm the lucky one. I love you, Sarah," Jerry said. We were holding hands on the couch.

"It's no different for me," I said. "I still wonder why you stick around when you get so fed up with me. Who would have thought the girl-next-door and the hippie would last this long?

"It's just funny sometimes how frustrated we get at each other, and then twenty minutes later, we are all over each other like white on rice, and I can't get enough. I remember the guys in the kitchen telling me to stay away from you, because I was just gonna have my heart broken," Jerry said with a smile.

"I know. I think about it and laugh. I want to go back to all those people and say, 'look at us now, you were all wrong.' Isn't it about time we go take showers?" I grabbed his hand and pulled him toward the bathroom

I got home from work one afternoon and Jerry was so eager to talk.

"So, momma, here's what I was thinking. The first painting I sold was of a naked woman in her bathroom, and I want to do another naked woman, but I want to try a live model. I already thought about all the details and what I would need to bring in the garage so you'd stay warm and be comfortable staying in the same position for a while. Baby, you know I love your curves, and you're beautiful. Will you model for me, please?"

"That sounds like it would be a lot of fun. What does momma get from daddy if I do this?" I replied.

"You know what you're going to get. It's more like what you're *not* going to get if I can't paint my sexy wife."

"Ha, ha! Of course, I will sit in a chair naked for you while you stare at me."

A few days later I was in the garage naked in a chair with a blanket. When he finished it, we both laughed. The body was great, but he needed help with faces. His first nude was the back view of a woman, but when I looked at the face of the new painting, it was very wrong. He said that in the future he wanted to take classes on painting portraits.

Jerry and I from day one had always been very courteous to each other with please and thank you, and always showing respect.

"Baby, thank you for doing all the laundry today. I could have helped," I said.

"You don't have to say thank you, it's my job," he replied.

"It's not your job, I live here too, and I can help."

"Do I say thank you to you for going to work every day?"

"No, but that's different, and I appreciate everything you do for me. Half the stuff you do around here, you don't have to," I said.

"Just stop saying thank you, it makes me feel like I'm your bitch, and I'm not your bitch," he said.

"Okay then," I responded

A Soulmates Twin Flame

Our conversation ended abruptly because I didn't know how to respond to that one. It had been a while, but it seemed like he was in a down mood that afternoon. I said thank you to him again a few days later, and he asked me to please stop. I felt awful not being able to let him know that I appreciated all he was doing. I tried to show him my appreciation in other ways.

The four of us spent Thanksgiving in 2014 with family up north. This time we flew; no more nightmare drives to New England. This trip, we saw snow, six inches of it. It was the most Brendan had ever seen, and he was excited to go sledding. Jerry and Brendan spent hours outside making snow angels on the ground, and a snowman. I watched most of the action from indoors and went out a few times playing photographer. Thanksgiving was spent at Jerry's mom's house. I was both happy and disappointed that we weren't home cooking together. I loved fooling around all day, but I didn't miss washing dishes. Jerry and I spent one night in a hotel while the kids were at his mom's. I was so excited. I would say he was too, it was his idea for a little alone time at night.

The night was spectacular. We lay in bed watching a movie on tv. After a few minutes I got a little closer and began kissing the back of his neck. He moved a little closer to me and I then slowly kissed my way down his chest. Jerry grabbed the remote, hit the off button, grabbed me, and pulled me closer. Then he slowly kissed me with a passion that drove me crazy, while caressing my body with his hands the whole time. I felt like there was this hidden magnetic force between us, constantly drawing us back together. We made slow passionate love and then finished the night was some intense, sweaty sex. It made the other evenings at my brother's house more difficult.

"Baby, stop, you can't be doing that right now. This is hard enough without you feeling me up and down," Jerry said.

"It's not easy for me either. We need to at least get closer, so we can snuggle," I said.

"Snuggle, you're funny, Momma. Your idea of snuggling is the best, but you need to turn down the playful tonight," he replied.

"Okay, but we can get close enough where you can hold me," I said sliding my hands down his chest and into his pants.

"Enough! This is not helping."

"I know, I can't help it. It's fun and you turn me on."

"Okay, honey, who gets turned on by fat and ugly?"

"Shut up," I said as my lips were exploring his waistline.

"I hear Brendan snoring," Jerry said. He was helping me get my clothes off under the blankets.

It was another great evening, except we had to be quieter than usual. Brendan was sleeping on an air mattress on the other side of the room, while Jerry and I shared a large sectional. The attraction I felt towards Jerry continued to grow, and I felt like I could never get enough. It was as simple as him walking into the room sometimes. I didn't say much out loud, but I would think to myself, *Holy shit, that gorgeous man is my husband. Wow, I just want to rip his clothes off. Fuck, he drives me crazy!*

Was it like this for all couples? I had no idea. I just knew what worked for us, what brought us joy. We had become inseparable over the years, and not intentionally. We didn't need to make friends or go out with other couples. We were enough for us.

Summer was almost here, and it had been a long year for Jerry with all the driving me and the kids back and forth. We decided to fix our truck, so Jerry could do things with the kids over the summer, and not worry about bringing me to work and picking me up. The truck had many minor issues. This was a project we were going to do together.

A Soulmates Twin Flame

"Alright momma, you know I need you for this one. I need your patience by my side while we take this apart and rebuild her. You know I don't do electrical; that's your job, and we got some serious issues there," Jerry said.

"Not a problem, baby, I love working by your side. You know this. I can be your gofer, and then you can be mine," I said.

We did most of it together. Jerry started while I was at work just taking everything apart and laying it on a tarp and covering it. We got to work the next morning.

"What the fuck! This is fucking bullshit! I'm so tired of being broke all the fucking time. I can't even buy fucking good tools. How am I supposed to do this with shit fucking tools!" Jerry yelled.

"It's not always the tools. I don't call you He-Man because I think it's cute. You always forget about your strength when you're pissed off, and ninety-nine percent of the time that's why shit gets broken or doesn't work right. Let me try please," I said.

"Fine, go right a fucking head."

"I didn't see what you were doing. Can you show me?"

Jerry then showed me what he was trying to reinstall, and I took over with the same tools.

"Why didn't you ask me for help? This is tight on my hands, and yours are twice the size. The tools worked fine. I think the problem was you not getting in close enough to tighten it," I said.

"You're right, I know. It's fucking stupid that you need tools, yet there's no room to use them. Thanks, Momma. This is why I said we needed to do this together. I'm learning, baby, I'm learning," Jerry said.

"Let's take a break, I want a smoke, and I'm hungry."

Sarah J Provost

The rest of the truck was easy. Jerry is a very smart man and knew everything that needed to be done and how to do it. He just needed a little more patience. When he couldn't get his hands in somewhere, he immediately asked me to help and see if I could. The next day we switched roles, and he stood by to help me while I found the electrical problem and re-did the wires and fuses. When all was done, we kissed each other and crossed our fingers that she would start, stay running and drive well. When she started right up, we laughed with happiness. There was nothing we couldn't do as a team.

A Soulmates Twin Flame

The Things We Learn

Fear and Jealousy

Jerry and I have had our issues, some were silly arguments that lasted ten minutes and then we were happy and playful again. Other times, not so easy. We had a battle that raged from jealousy on both our ends, but I started it.

Jerry and I were sitting on the couch one night, talking about his painting, specifically how he wanted to paint love themes that included naked women. He was searching for pictures that showed love and passion in the faces of the women, or the position they were in. This didn't bother me, or so I thought.

But while scrolling on our computer, I clicked on a picture of a half-naked man, and not just any man. This was a sexy underwear model man. My sister called, and I left the image on the screen for the whole five minutes I was talking while Jerry was right beside me. I hung up, looked at the computer and clicked off the image. Jerry was very quiet and normally would ask me what my sister was up to or how she was. He didn't say a word that night until it was time for bed.

"I'm going to take my shower and get ready for bed. Are you coming, my love?" I asked.

"No, I'm not tired," he replied.

"I'm not tired either. We don't go into the bedroom this early for sleep. Are you coming?" I asked

"No, I'm working on something right now."

"Okay, I'll meet you in there."

I went into the bedroom, took my time picking out clothes for work in the morning and sat on the bed for a few minutes with still no Jerry. This was extremely odd, because even when he was actually in the middle of something, he threw it aside as soon as he watched me walk into the bedroom. He was pissed, alright. Was that the reaction I was looking for all along? It was Jerry's job to research naked women, and I had nothing to be insecure about. In fact, I checked the history on our computer and saw that he scanned hundreds of pictures at a time, all in about a minute. So, me staring at the underwear model was harmless too, right?

I walked back out into the living room half undressed and asked him again if he was going to join me. He threw his sketch pad down and said fine. We went into the bedroom and Jerry wouldn't even look at me.

"What is your problem?" I asked.

"Nothing. Are you getting in the shower? if not then I'm getting in," he said in a very irritated tone.

"Something is wrong, what is it?"

"I said nothing!"

"Jerry, there is something wrong. Talk to me."

"Alright, fine, you want to know what's what wrong. It's you! You're going to sit here and tell me you love me, how gorgeous you think your husband is, and then stare at naked men online while I'm right next to you. You're a fucking liar! Don't fucking talk to me anymore."

"Are you kidding me? You're mad at that one picture? You have no right to get mad at me when you spend your mornings looking at naked women while I'm at work."

"Are you my fucking mother now, checking up on me? You are unbelievable. I can't stand you, I don't even want to look at you anymore. Don't fucking say another word to me!" He yelled and then started to walk into the bathroom.

"Jerry, I don't understand how you could be mad at that one picture. I know I was wrong for checking the history. I'm sorry."

"Do you not understand fucking English! I said don't fucking talk to me anymore. You won't even listen. We're done!"

"We're not done, you're not gonna quit that easy over something stupid," I said. Jerry grabbed a pillow and walked towards the door.

"You just keep opening your mouth. I want a fucking divorce. You say another fucking word and I am leaving tonight. Leave me alone! We will talk tomorrow!"

I don't know if we woke up the kids or not, but they didn't come out of their rooms. I sat on the bed for a few hours crying, while Jerry sat on the couch in darkness. I grabbed a pack of cigarettes and a bottle of water and walked the neighborhood for a few hours When I got home, Jerry was still sitting there in the darkness, staring at nothing. I sat on the bed again for another hour until it was time to get the kids up for school. I drove them to school, went back home and called in sick to work. Jerry still hadn't moved, and I was not about to talk to him. I went and sat outside and spent the day out near our fire pit. I walked back into the house and told myself it was time to say something. We only had an hour until it was time to pick the kids up from school.

"Jerry are you ready to talk now?" I said peacefully

"I told you to come and talk to me today," he replied.

That's not what I understood from what he said last night. I had been waiting all day for him to tell me he was ready to talk.

"I don't want you to leave, I'm sorry, I was wrong for checking the history, I knew what you were doing and why. I don't know why I was jealous. I know you're in love with me," I said.

"Sarah, I apologize for screaming like that. That in itself was wrong. I spent the entire night thinking and trying to figure out why I got so mad at that one picture. It seems like nothing, but to me, it was a big deal. I am so in love with you. I fear every day that you will find someone better. You deserve better, and I know this, and someday you will figure that out too, I just don't know when. I have never felt jealousy like this until you. I was so hurt that you looked at another man. I want to be the man that you always desire and look at. Sarah, I'm sorry. I tried to tell you nothing last night because I didn't want to scream at you and needed to calm down before I said anything. You kept on pushing and my mouth got the best of me. I don't want a divorce. I don't ever want to lose you," he said.

"Jerry, it's ok. I thought about that too. You have told me over and over that you need time to think and get your thoughts straight before you talk, but you know I'm the opposite and need to talk immediately. You spent the night thinking. I spent the night worrying, and the silence between us was excruciatingly painful. We were both wrong, and we are both jealous. I don't and will never desire another man. I would think you'd realize this by now, but then again, I was no different. I love you more than anything and you know this," I said. I moved closer and wrapped my arms around him. I couldn't take it any longer. I wanted to feel his arms around me.

We both picked up the kids from school. That night there wasn't a lot of talking, but we decided to watch a movie together instead of working in his studio. Jerry had his arms around me the entire time, and I could periodically feel him hold on tighter. Later that night we went into the bedroom together, showered, snuggled and made love like we usually do. The lovemaking was quite intense. I always felt a deep emotional connection between us, but this went further. Erased were Jerry's threats to divorce me. Gone was the jealousy, at least for a little while.

Jerry and I had another Incident on a Saturday afternoon after house cleaning. Many times, when it's late in the day we'd stop at McDonald's on our way home to get dinner. I always go in, and he waits in the car. Normally we just get dinner for the kids, but periodically it's for all four of us. I ordered a good amount of food that day, and they put everything in this large paper bag. It was no cheap paper bag either. I walked out and looked at Jerry with a big smile, flashing my fancy paper bag thinking I was special. I looked to see if any cars were coming and crossed the parking lot and got back into the car. I told Jerry while we were driving that I was a special and was given the fancy paper bag.

We all ate dinner together, and normally Jerry is all smiles telling the kids about our day and joking around. Not that day. He still talked with them a little, but it wasn't in his normal upbeat tone. After dinner, I made us coffee, and we got ready to veg out and relax because we were both beat from a long day. Jerry was still quieter than he normally is and usually, I have some inclination of what could be wrong, but not that time. I analyzed the whole day over and over so many times trying to figure out why he was down. We were happy and laughing all day even while cleaning up gross houses. I was already extremely close to him, so I just put my around him and kissed his cheek thinking that would bring out a smile. Nope, I was wrong there.

"Jerry are you ok tonight? Is something wrong or are you not feeling good?" I asked.

"I'm fine," he said.

"Okay, I love you baby," I said as I kissed his cheek again and grabbed his hand.

Jerry didn't hold my hand with the strength and desire like he normally would. I could feel that something was wrong and I thought maybe it was something with me, but I had no clue what, or why.

"Baby are you sure you're ok? you seem a little distant tonight," I asked.

"When are you going to just tell me you're leaving me?" He blurted out.

"What? What are you talking about?" I asked in complete shock.

"When are you going to tell me, you're leaving me!" He said again.

"I'm sorry, but I don't know what you're talking about,"

"I know you're going to just leave me. I saw you today while we were at McDonald's flirting with the two guys in the parking lot that were checking you out. You turned your head and smiled right at them," He said.

"What guys? What are you talking about?"

"So, you're going to sit here and lie to my face that you weren't flirting with those guys?"

"What guys? I don't understand what you're talking about," I said as I was trying to stay calm but was about ready to blow my top because I was clueless and did not do anything wrong.

"You're a liar, just leave me alone, please. I need time," He said as he walked outside and went to the garage.

"NO! don't you fucking walk away from me!" I screamed as I was pissed, to say the least.

I followed him outside to the garage and he again asked for some time alone, so he could think, he said he didn't want to yell. He then closed the garage door before I got there.

"I am so tired of this shit. I can't believe how insecure you are, and I can't fucking take it any longer. You're gonna get mad at me for something that I didn't do, call me a liar, and expect me to give you time. Well, Fuck you! Jerry, I don't think I can do this any longer. I can only take so much, and you won't even try to explain. I hope you're fucking happy!" I screamed through the door.

As I was about to walk away he opened the garage door.

"Sarah, can you please come in here, so we can talk?" He asked

"Talk, about what? What is there to talk about? You saw something that wasn't there, let your mind create a story, blamed me for something that I am completely clueless about. There is nothing to talk about unless you want to know what I saw when I walked out of McDonald's."

"Sarah, I'm sorry. I get scared sometimes that I'm going to lose you, and when I see men staring at my wife, I don't like it. Your beautiful with a huge heart and any man would be lucky to have you. I feel that you deserve a man who's not a loser like me. I don't know what you saw when you walked out, obviously, it wasn't what I saw. I have never seen this anger from you, nor the complete dumbfounded look because you really didn't know. I didn't mean to call you a liar, that's why I needed to ask for time alone, so I didn't say anything foolish."

"Can I tell you what I saw now? Are you done? Number one, you're not a loser. Jerry, all I saw was my husband. I thought I was all that and a bag of chips showing you my paper bag with a smile as I walked to the car. All I saw was you and stared into your eyes. I looked to the side to check for cars, but you know what, I couldn't even tell you if there were or not. I was so fixated on you and it was a habit to turn and look. I never even knew there were people outside when I walked out. I saw no one except you. I was so happy to see you waiting for me and was in my lovey daydream state that you were all I paid attention to."

"I realized that you never even saw the guys standing outside by how clueless and pissed you were. I have said to you before that you need to pay attention to your surroundings, but this was extreme. Those guys were right next to you checking you out, and you saw none of it. Sarah, that scares me. Too often you don't pay attention, and that's dangerous."

"I know all of this, and you're right about the paying attention, but why didn't you just ask me if I saw them, or ask me who I was smiling at? It's that easy, that's what I don't understand. This argument was for no reason."

"Momma, I'm so sorry. Please forgive me. I should have never said that you were a liar, I was just hurt, and scared that you were looking for another man."

"I don't know what more I can do, to show you how much I am in love with you. Jerry, I don't even have fun unless you're by my side. We do everything together. I'm just confused at how you come up with these stories sometimes."

"I don't know, but I promise you that I will ask questions. I will try my best to calm the mind, but if I create stories I will ask and not jump to conclusions. I'm sorry, I love you baby!

"God knows how much I love you, and so does everyone else for that matter. I really wish you knew too."

"Baby, I do know, I do," he said as he hugged me.

The weirdest thing about that argument, was even though Jerry was mad, hurt, and thought he was being lied to, he didn't yell or raise his voice. I, on the other hand, have never screamed at him like that before. After our talk, I had thoughts that kept racing through my head. I realized that I only have eyes for Jerry, and that will never change. I look into his eyes and it's all over. I then feel like I'm living a dream, and nothing matters any longer. I get mesmerized and can't help but stare at him. There have been times when I look at him, and there's that old saying about when your heart melts or skips a beat. Let me be the one to tell you, it's not just a saying. I have literally felt that with Jerry with something as simple as walking into the room with his beautiful smile.

A Soulmates Twin Flame

The other thing I realized that was a little scary, was the fact that there were two guys standing right next to me, looking at me and I didn't see anyone. They could have had a gun pointed at me and I would not have seen it. I need to pay more attention to what's around me and get out of my dream world when we're together.

Sarah J Provost

Creative Sexy Romance
Love is open and playful

Jerry and I had always been very passionate, playful, and affectionate towards each other. We had spent many evenings researching photos online that he could you use as references for a series of passion and love paintings that he wanted to do. Jerry told me he was very specific to facial expression and body language. We were unsuccessful in our research.

"Momma, I haven't found anything yet that shows what I'm looking for, and neither have you. Baby, we have such an intense passion and love. What if we made our own photos?"

"What do you mean by our own photos?" I asked

"Well, we could set up the camera on any evening, and just be us. The look I see in your face is exactly what I am trying to find. Your body and curves are fucking amazing, and I would love to work from an image of my girl."

"Alright, that sounds like fun, and I know better now what you're looking for. I see the same expressions in your face, but for me, it's the eyes. Your eyes say so much. Baby, that's a great idea. I love it!"

A few nights later we set up the camera in our bedroom on interval shooting and the camera took a photo every minute. Jerry and I didn't change anything that we normally did and enjoyed each other. I forgot the camera was taking photos until we got up to go outside for a smoke. The camera caught every intimate moment: the way we kissed each other, the way he caressed my body, and us making love. There were over one hundred photos, with many of them showing exactly what Jerry was looking for. After that night Jerry came up with more ideas for photo shoots, a few for paintings and some just because it was fun. He said the photos were beautiful and showed real love between two people.

For one photo shoot labeled as light stripes, Jerry removed the door from the closet and hung up a room-darkening mini blind. He turned on the closet light and opened the blinds just enough to allow the light to make stripes on my body. That night he played photographer for a little while and took many different photos of me naked with stripes on my body from the light. Then he put the camera on a tripod and set up the interval shooting. Jerry and I were both naked and the camera caught photos of us kissing, holding each other, and a few of me sitting on Jerry's lap. Jerry loved the effect and wanted to do the stripes again. The next night he covered my body head-to-toe in baby oil and played photographer again. The reflection of the light and the shimmer on my body really made them stand out, and I had fun. It took a little while to wash off all the baby oil after, and then we had a very intense night, but we shut the camera off for that. Before long, Jerry came up with a few more ideas.

"Ok momma, what do you think about a tub photo shoot, with glowing red water?" he asked.

"I like that idea, but how will you do it? Will it be both of us in the tub or just me?"

"It will be just you. I want more photos of my beautiful wife. Baby, you have curves that drive me crazy. You know our red rope light?"

"Yeah, what about it?"

"That's what we're going to use. Don't worry, I will make it safe so we can plug it in and submerge it in the water. We are also going to use some cornstarch after to make the water look creamy, and then I will only see the parts of you that are not submerged. Momma, I think these will be really beautiful photos."

"I'm excited! We can do it tonight if you want to take a night away from us working."

Jerry got everything ready, and we took pictures that evening. I had fun posing for him in the tub. I knew by his smile, laughter and the way he was looking at me that he was having a great time. He brought a chair in the bathroom so he could have a few views from above looking down at me. He took many photos and then asked me to get out. I got out thinking he was done taking pictures, but he kept shooting, so we have some funny pictures of me naked with the main light on. You could see every detail in those last few pictures. He put the camera down, pulled me close to him and kissed me. My towel fell to the floor and he gently ran his hands down my body. We stood in the bathroom for another minute or two, and then we were on the edge of the bed together. An hour later, we got dressed to go outside for a few minutes. I hardly called this work!

Jerry and I did other photo shoots together, some for references and others just for fun. Jerry said he loved photography and playing naked with his wife.

Another night Jerry said he wanted to do a painting of just a woman, but he wanted her wearing lingerie and to be wet. That night Jerry pulled out a few outfits for me to wear in the shower. As difficult as it was to change my clothes under running water, I had fun. Jerry laughed most of the time, as he saw how much I struggled to change while he was taking the pictures. In another shower scene we were both naked and took turns with the camera. He photographed me with different body parts pressed against the glass shower door. Some were with just running water and others with bubbles. Then Jerry took his shower with me photographing him. We had a level of trust and comfort that let us be ourselves with each other whether that was silly, crazy, or just different. We were very open and always willing to experiment with one another.

A Soulmates Twin Flame

Jerry wasn't feeling well one night and asked me to *please* do something and make him smile. We were already naked in bed, and I did the first thing that popped into my head. I jumped out of bed and started dancing, first a ballet dance, then I took it up a notch and showed him a few tap dance moves. I was dancing all around the room with a lot of jumping up and down. He was laughing so hard that he had tears in his eyes.

"Momma, you're awesome! That was fucking awesome. Did you hear that?" Jerry said. He was laughing so hard he could hardly speak.

"Hear what?" I asked.

"Your boobs, they're clapping when you jump. Wow! You are good at titty clapping!"

"Thank you, baby!" I said and then continued to jump so he'd cry again with laughter.

"Baby, I fucking love you! You are really good at that, you know."

"I'm not twenty anymore, so it's easy when you got so much that shakes and jiggles."

I laid back down in bed with Jerry and his huge smile. He thanked me again and told me how funny I was and how much he loved me. Jerry and I had become more open and experimental over the years sometimes playing with sex toys. Having pure fun sex on some nights made the lovemaking even more intense. We were outside having a smoke before our sleep time talking and Jerry always knew what to say to make me feel special.

"Baby, I never knew I could feel like this. Our love is incredible. There is nothing I like more than making love to my wife. Our toys are fun, but when it's just our bodies and the way we touch each other and look at each other, it's like magic. I still get butterflies when you kiss me, even after all these years," Jerry said.

"See, I knew you felt it too. You laughed when I told you I still felt the butterflies, but that laugh sounded more like a *Wow! You too?* kind of laugh, rather than you laughing at me. Jerry, you make me feel that way every day, and you have for quite some time," I replied and kissed him on his cheek.

Jerry made a movie of us one evening. He remembered an old video camera that had night vision and filmed while I was getting undressed. You can hear us laughing and talking about how the night vision gave my body a bright glow, while Jerry stumbled through the dark. After a few more minutes, I asked to have the camera so I could see what he looked like in night vision and filmed him while sitting naked on the bed. Jerry laughed, trying to act sexy, and slowly took his clothes off as he sang, 'Bringing Sexy Back.' He turned around and was surprised that I filmed his whole routine.

"Can you still see me?" Jerry asked. He was walking into the bathroom.

"Oh yeah! Do the elephant dance for me please, and the windmill," I asked.

I was laughing and still recording him while he grabbed his toothbrush. He saw that the red light was on and started dancing and singing while brushing his teeth.

"Bringing sexy back, while I brush my teeth," he sang.

Jerry and Brendan were in the front yard throwing around a football one afternoon. As Jerry ran, my eyes were fixated on his front package. He was wearing a gray pair of sweatpants, and every time he moved, they formed to his body. Out of the blue, I started singing:

"What are you gonna do with all that junk, all that junk in your front!" Jerry laughed, looked down and then smiled at me seductively.

"I know what I'm saving these pants for," he said.

I also found his construction boots sexy. Yep, you read that right! One afternoon I watched him working in the yard, strutting around in his boots and sweating, and I couldn't wait for him to come in the house. I followed him into the bedroom and helped get those clothes off in a hurry and got on my knees. That lasted less than a minute, and he got me up and pulled me close, kissed me while taking my clothes off and pushed me down on the bed. Those middle of the day, sexy I-have-to-have-you-now moments couldn't be beat. For all of his charm and sex appeal, Jerry could be a complete asshole too. I was in love with the whole package.

A few of our intimate moments

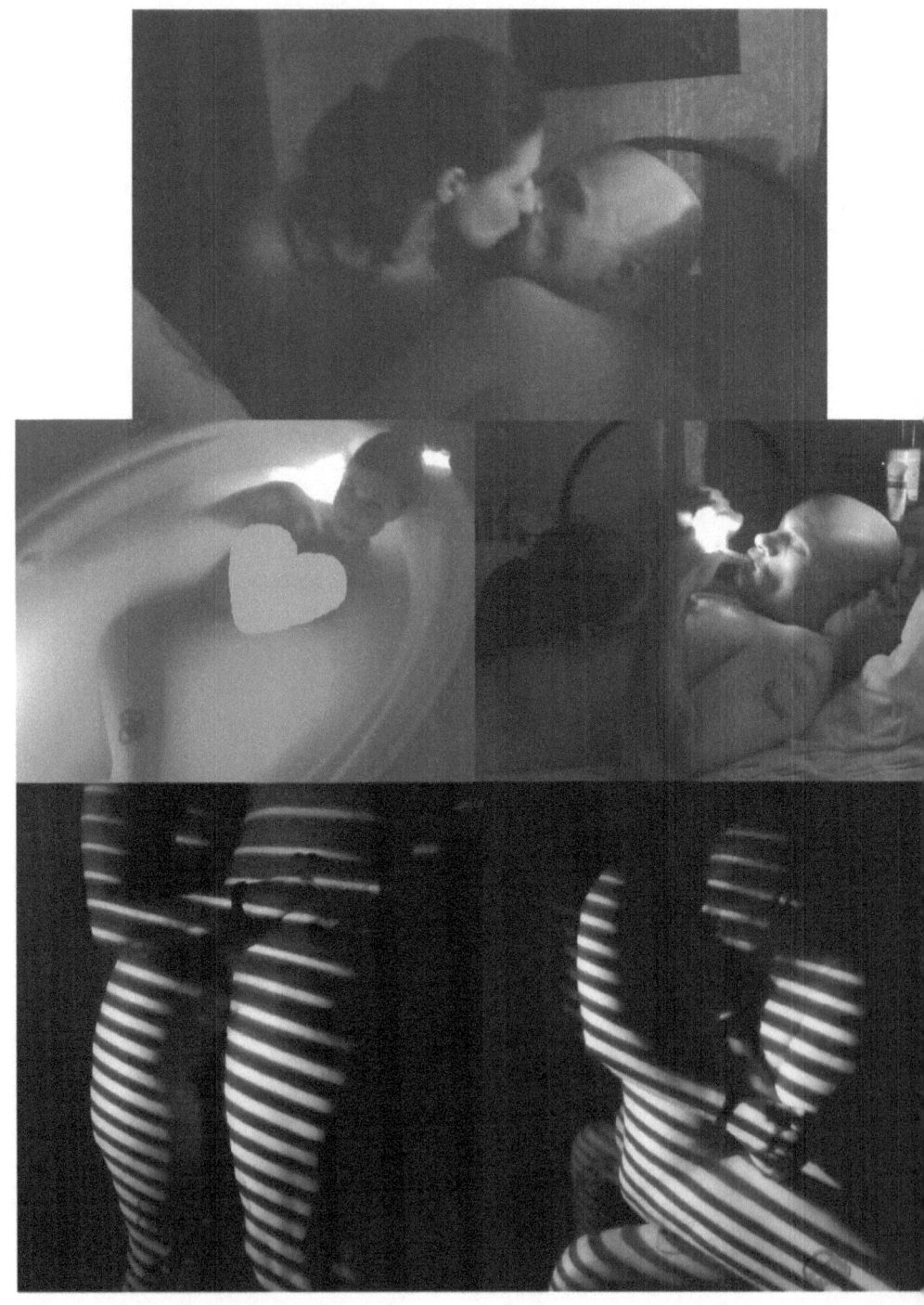

A Soulmates Twin Flame

Excitement Awaits

Hooray for Love

As Jerry continued to work on his paintings he said online sales were not enough, mainly because his work couldn't be priced as high as that of a known artist. We decided that his participation in local art festivals would be a great way to gain exposure for his artwork. Just as Jerry was getting ready for this art festival, he received his first custom order that was strictly on the merits of his website. Custom jobs for friends and friends of friends or co-workers were wonderful. But this job came from someone who fell in love with Jerry's style online. We were thrilled!

The new client was a woman who wanted to surprise her husband with a military painting that was personal to him. Once completed she left him a five-star review. A few other custom orders followed via his website and all resulted in five-star reviews. There was nothing I could do to wipe the smile from his face after that first order. He was finally starting to have more confidence in his work.

Our first art festival was in October of 2015. We set up on Friday and watched a beautiful sunrise over the ocean the next morning as we put the finishing touches on our display. We noticed that, with all the early morning dew, water was dripping down the tent and getting the paintings wet. There was no damage done, but it was a pain in the ass to keep wiping the paintings down every few minutes. We were amateurs compared to everyone else at the show. An artist next to us gave us some great tips for future shows. Jerry was excited, but also nervous about so many people looking at his art.

"Knock it off," I told him. "Your work is gorgeous, just like you."

We sold ten paintings, made our money back for the cost of the show, plus some. Jerry received many compliments on his art. After that first show, he said he couldn't wait for the next one.

In the fall, Jerry completed the passion painting that he did from one of our photos. It sold right away; we were both astonished. A few days after I shipped the painting to the buyer, another client asked for a passion painting. While Jerry was working on a second passion painting, the woman bought two more paintings and left five star reviews. A week later, I saw that she had bought three more! I was at work and counted down the minutes until five, so I could tell Jerry. I didn't want to call him, because I wanted to see the look on his face.

"Hey, baby! So, I have something I need to tell you," I said.

"What is it, what happened?"

"Baby, you need to sit down for this one, and no, I'm not leaving you, so just wipe that thought right out of your head," I said, laughing.

"Alright then, what is it?" he asked.

"Okay, you know the lady that asked you to paint another passion painting and then bought two different paintings?"

"Yeah, what about her?"

"Well, we got an order today and she purchased three more paintings."

"Are you fucking kidding me?" Jerry jumped right out of his chair.

"No baby, I'm not kidding, three more paintings gone!"

Jerry asked which ones she bought, and I removed them from the walls, so I could get them packed and ready to ship. He couldn't stop pacing, then ran to tell the kids that three more of his pieces of art were off to California.

"This is so fucking awesome, now we can go and buy more canvas. I didn't know what I was going to do. I'm running low on canvas. I need a few new colors too," he said.

"I love you, baby, and your smile!" I said.

Within another week, he finished the passion painting and the new client purchased the painting along with another one. I again was so excited and couldn't wait to get home and tell Jerry. He was dumbfounded, and I got the same, "Are you fucking kidding me?" Jerry's excitement level that night was wonderful and contagious. Another week went by and he sold two more paintings. He again ran to the kids and told them that one of his paintings was off to Hawaii, and hopefully his art would be in every state soon enough.

"Momma, thank you!" Jerry said that night as his arms were wrapped around me.

"For what?" I asked

"For loving me the way you do and everything you do for me every day. You are my passion and my inspiration. My best work is done when I paint my feelings after our passionate nights. Those passion paintings have been my favorite. I'm expressing my love for you and letting the world see," he said.

"You're welcome and thank you for loving me. I still don't know what I did, but I'm loving your affection."

"Baby, if it wasn't for you, we would have never known about festivals and you created the whole store and did everything to get my name out there. All I did was paint."

"I liked doing it, and for me it was fun. This art is for us and our future. I know you have your doubts still, but I don't. Remember, baby, we both said that within seven to eight years your art will be supporting us, and I can quit my job. Then we can spend all day together."

"I know, I want to make it happen quicker. It's awesome when you're working beside me."

I agreed. The time for us to spend every day together was on the horizon, and I couldn't wait. The excitement made our already great nights even better. Occasionally we fell asleep while snuggling when one of us wasn't feeling good, but other than not, we played. Nothing stopped our playtime, not a single day of the month. Jerry said to me one night,

"If you can't be open, honest, and gross with your spouse, then who can you be that way with? I'm going to take another shower baby, this requires a little more than a sponge bath."

I didn't really know what to say other than okay, and I laughed with him.

An Amazing Husband

For the love of Art

Sleeping was never something Jerry was good at, averaging only about three to four hours a night. Even that became a struggle as the voices in his head grew louder. The more he expressed himself through his art, the more voices he heard and the more ideas he had. At least that's how he explained it to me. As his business grew, he had three painting easels going. He'd be working on one painting, and then an idea would come into his head for something he needed to add to the other painting. His impatience was also a factor. He enjoyed painting so much that he didn't want to wait for a certain area of his work to dry so he could paint again. He had multiples going and never had to put down his brush.

I continued booking us at art festivals, and those usually went well. Jerry was beginning to get frustrated and thought he should be making more money. I tried to explain that through all my research, it seemed that most artists didn't sell a single piece of work for many years. Jerry was still battling his insecurities about not being able to support his family financially. His impatient personality would sometimes get the best of him.

I reminded Jerry of the ten paintings he sold in a month and the great income boost that gave us. He wanted to see that every month. I said one day we will. He still always tried to make sure he was doing his 'job' as he called it, which was maintaining the house. I tried to help, but he always had everything done before I got home from work.

Every once in a blue moon I would offer to make dinner. That meant a lot to him. He knew how much I hated cooking, and for a trained chef no less.

"I don't know what to make for dinner that will be any good," I said.

"Momma, anything you make is good. I like grandma's home cooking type of meals. I didn't get this big for nothing," he said.

"Knock it off, you're not big, and you know it!" I replied.

"I was big when I was younger, and it wasn't because I didn't like my mom's cooking."

"Yeah I know, but you also weren't a chef yet back then."

"Do you know how much it sucks to eat every night. Everything I make, I have made so many times that I can taste it before I eat. I don't even like eating anymore. No one cooks the same. You can make the same recipe and it will be different from the way mine came out. It's awesome for me to eat something and not know all the flavors before it gets to my mouth. Make anything you want, momma. I'll eat it."

"Ok, if you say so, I'll try"

I have gotten a little better at cooking over the years, but I have only done it a handful of times. I will never forget my first time making dinner for the family. It was a disaster and awful. I followed a recipe and made pork chops, but they turned out to be bricks. You couldn't cut one, but you could knock someone out cold if you hit them with it. The kids begged Jerry to get a pizza and not make them eat mom's food.

Every night after dinner Jerry and I would clean up the dinner mess together, holding hands whenever we were close enough. Once the kids left the kitchen, it was playtime mixed with cleaning. Every time I walked by him, I would reach out and grab him or kiss him. Many times, I would drop something and bend over right in front of him and pick it up. He would smack my ass or wrap his hands around my waist and pretend while he rubbed against me for a second or two. Sometimes the kids would see us. They thought we were crazy and just shook their heads. Crazy in love, I was.

A Soulmates Twin Flame

Jerry and I still had our disagreements, but we argued less about the kids as the years went by. I had gotten better about addressing their disrespectfulness, and he didn't yell like he used to. As parents, we achieved a balance that other people seemed to notice.

We were complimented many times on the kid's behavior, their kindness, and their manners by people who knew us and by strangers who had just met them. Jerry said he'd never forget when he picked Brendan up from school one day and a teacher told him that she wished she could clone our son and only have Brendan's in her class because he was the best student she had ever had. We both thought she went a little overboard, but regardless it was wonderful to hear. Things would go so well with us as a family, and with me and Jerry as a couple. Then, out of nowhere, one of Jerry's demons would walk in the room.

We were in the studio together. Jerry was painting, and I was putting up a few new paintings for sale.

"You would be better off if I just left," he blurted out suddenly.

"What? What are you talking about?" I asked

"No one talks to me anymore, not you, not the kids."

"Jerry, I'm confused. What are you talking about?"

"No one talks to me. The kids don't say anything. You and I don't talk like we used to. You deserve better, not a loser like me."

"Oh my God, would you knock it off. The kids are getting older, and they don't talk to me either, so you can just stop with that shit. I don't know what to tell you about us. Baby, we don't leave the house, so yeah, some days there is less to talk about than others. I'm ok with not talking every moment, you're not. Why don't you try calling a friend and spend a little while catching up?

"Yeah, I could, I don't know. Sometimes I just feel like you don't want to be here anymore because you don't always talk to me."

"I love talking to you about anything, but I don't always know what to talk about. You're good at coming up with the crazy shit for us to talk about," I said.

"I know, but why does it always have to be me to start the conversation?"

"The last time I tried to talk about something different and be creative, you looked at me like I had four eyes and showed no interest, so I said so much for that idea. I know you need conversation all the time, and I tried. My mind is just not as imaginative as yours. Why don't we try and go out for a ride one night? You know we always talk and laugh when we see new stuff."

"We could, but I want to help you be more creative. I didn't mean to make you think I had no interest, but I was in the middle of something."

"That's another thing that sometimes makes it a little harder. I have to wonder about my timing. You don't worry about that with me. No matter what I am doing you come first, and I would stop anything just to listen to you. You are not as simple. Baby, I am never going anywhere. I am in love with you, and you know this. So just stop, please."

"I know you love me, momma. My mind sometimes takes over, and I fear the worst. I love you so much, but I do still get scared that one day you're gonna find a real man that can support you and has a job."

"Please shut-up now. I love you, you're crazy, and I need to finish putting your painting up for sale, so we can snuggle and play," I said as I walked over, sat on his lap and kissed him.

Jerry and I finished what we were working on and went upstairs to tell the kids it was time for bed. All his thoughts of me being better off without him fell by the wayside. We closed out the world for the night and entered our Jerry and Sarah bubble of love.

Jerry told me about an artist he admired. He said his work was very unique and each picture told a story about the love he had for his wife. Jerry said this artist and his wife locked themselves in their house, everything they needed was delivered, and they lived alone, just the two of them. They would spend most days naked, running around their house, in a relationship built on unconditional love and desire. Jerry said that this artist lived every day with so much happiness.

"Baby, that's going to be us, I know it. When the kids grow up, and it's back to just me and you, that's exactly what it will be like for us. I can't wait," I said with a huge smile.

"I know it will, momma, that's why I told you about them. I can't wait. I love you Sarah," he replied.

We have had conversations about our future, our plans, and our dreams. One dream we had was having our own boat that we could live on if we chose. For our fifteenth wedding anniversary, Jerry painted me a beach scene that had our boat in the water, and he painted a name on and called it "Our Love Boat." There were also two chairs and flowers on the beach. I also received a love letter. I was in tears when I saw the painting and read my letter.

Before the year ended, I took Jerry with me to the doctor's office. I had a hemorrhoid that was a blood clot, and it needed to be surgically removed.

"I can't believe you're gonna show your cheeks for another man," Jerry said, trying to make me laugh.

"Ha, ha, smart ass. I know you're trying to get me to smile. You're here with me, that's all I need. But I'm not smiling," I said.

When the doctor told me, I would feel a pinch, he lied. It was way worse than a pinch. Jerry was kneeling next to me, looking into my eyes, and holding both of my hands. Afterwards, I was afraid to sit for the first day or two. Jerry and I did not know how to ask the doctor about sex, so Jerry became my doctor and checked to see how I was healing. Jerry said he could take pictures, so I could see.

"Alright momma, bend over and spread 'em," he said, laughing.

"Can you see it?" I asked

"No, pull your cheeks apart," he asked.

"Ok, is that better, just take a picture already please," I said.

"Alright, baby the lighting sucks, put a leg up on the sink. Ok, try and turn more towards the light. Alright, now try and bend a little more but keep your leg up there. Try and twist a little more towards the light."

"Is that better? Take the picture, please, so I can see," I said.

"I got a few, but they're really dark; don't move yet. Alright, momma, turn a little more towards the light."

"Ok I need to move now; I'm not a contortionist, alright maybe a little, but this is ridiculous. You just want to see how much I can move and bend. That's why you haven't stopped laughing," I said to him.

"Baby you come really close to a contortionist. I love it. My wife is fucking awesome. I got a good one, baby. You can move now," he said, laughing his ass off.

"Thank you, I want to see the pictures."

Jerry checked for a few more days, and I was all healed with no problems. I had my own photo fun when Jerry had a problem in a location he couldn't see and wanted to know what it looked like. I got some really great close-ups. Jerry said he was going to do an abstract painting of the picture I took. It was of the underside of his nuts. If you didn't know that's what I took a picture of, you wouldn't guess it. Jerry and I laughed when we uploaded all the photos to the computer. We didn't realize how many pictures we had of ourselves naked, certain body parts, our photo shoots, and my numerous random photos of him doing crazy things. We laughed a lot going through them and said we needed to make sure the kids never had access to our computer.

A Soulmates Twin Flame

The hemorrhoid story was only significant because of Jerry. When the doctor told me to expect a pinch, I saw such a pain in Jerry's eyes, like he could feel it. He had tears in his eyes before I did, and I was the one on the table. When we were driving home, he tried to explain a weird feeling that went through him and how he could feel physical pain when he looked at me. I told Jerry to stop trying to explain because I knew what he was talking about and I understood. Jerry had always thought it was incredible that a mother could feel her child's pain. But it surprised him that he could feel my pain, and he already knew I could feel his.

Christmas of 2015 was special because Jerry and I bought each other gifts, something we had not done in many years. Jerry received plenty of new and different canvases along with new paints. He was so excited and asked if Christmas was almost over, so he could get back to work. Jerry and the kids bought me a new digital photo frame and a new camera bag. I loved it and looked forward to converting all my pictures to digital.

That Christmas we also flew his mom down as a surprise for the kids. I left early from work one afternoon to pick her up at the airport. She waited in Jerry's studio, and I told the kids Daddy wanted to talk to them. When they saw their grandma sitting there, Isabelle started crying and Brendan was happy too. It was a great Provost family Christmas that year. We had so much to be thankful for.

Provost Family Christmas

A Soulmates Twin Flame

Just the Two of Us
Feel the flutter from Love

Every night we celebrated Jerry and Sarah. Once we said goodnight to the kids, it was all about us, two or three uninterrupted hours alone together in our bedroom. I would get into my 'parking spot' as Jerry called it, with my head resting on his chest and his arm around me. We'd gaze into each other's eyes and exchange passionate kisses.

After a little while, I would rest my head on his stomach in a way where he could see the rest of my body. That was when he would smoke his marijuana, and I inhaled its sweet perfume. While he was smoking he would caress my body, and I would his, until he was done smoking, and I kissed his lips again. The passion was intense, and the butterflies in my stomach were something I craved every day.

When our bodies would connect, it still didn't feel close enough for me. The emotions and all the overwhelming sensations were crazy. After lovemaking, we'd stand up and meet in the center of the room. We were like odd birds in a mating ritual. We'd stand there, look into each other's eyes, he would then grab me, pull me close and hug me. Sometimes we danced.

"I don't want to let you go," I said as he held me in the middle of the room.

"Sarah, we are two perfect fit puzzle pieces," he said.

"Baby, you're amazing, and I love you," I replied.

Jerry would hold me until I fell asleep, which never took long. Jerry had a nickname for me, he called me his 'Pfizer'.

"Baby, you are the best drug in the world, and I'm addicted," he said.

I have called him my He-Man, along with daddy, my love, or baby. It was rare when we used each other's names. Jerry called me momma more than anything else. I told Jerry many times that he was He-Man, and he would laugh and say I was crazy.

We were out shopping with the kids at the mall one afternoon and I saw a 'She-Ra' bra and panty set.

"Baby come here! Look what I found," I said.

"What is it, momma?" he asked.

"Look, a 'She-Ra' bra and panty set. You're my He-Man, and now I am your She-Ra."

I had to have it. I thought it was perfect and couldn't wait to put it on and show him when we got home.

By the time we got home, Jerry tried his best to annoy me with his negativity. I told him I had plans later for my sexy man.

"If he's so sexy, then maybe should go be with him," he replied.

"Oh my God, shut-up. Let me rephrase that. Jerry, my husband, is sexy."

"Momma take my glasses; obviously you need them more than I do. We need to get your vision checked," he said.

"Okay, you know what? I don't know why I bother. You wonder why no one talks to you. Jerry, you're gorgeous and you know I think that, so knock it off," I said.

Jerry and I were never afraid of public displays of affection. We held hands everywhere, and I would kiss him in front of anyone. All too often we had been inappropriate walking around stores. I would reach out and grab him right in the front.

"They just saw you grab me," he said, smiling.

"Yeah, so, your point?" I kissed him, and he grabbed my ass.

"See, that old lady watched me grab your ass," Jerry said.

"Let's see if she continues to watch," I said, running my hands under his shirt.

"Yes, she's still watching, and you need to stop, or we are going to have to go home now."

"Okay, fine. Look, she's smiling. I bet she likes seeing people in love."

Jerry was great at making me laugh. There had been multiple nights where the laughter was non-stop, and I had to ask him to please stop because my cheeks were hurting. He cracked up every time I had to tell him my cheeks were hurting. Jerry put a post on his Facebook art page one morning that read, "Over eighteen years together, and I still make her cheeks hurt. Now that is an awesome love!"

For Jerry's 45th birthday, I wanted to surprise him with flowers, what he called Mother Nature's most beautiful creations. Jerry had never been typical, and I certainly couldn't just surprise him with roses. With the help of a local florist, I picked out a square vase brimming with flowers, all perfect for Jerry: sunflowers, orchids, oriental lilies, tiger lilies (he loved their orange color), a few roses, Hawaiian birds of paradise, and a few other tropical flowers.

During my lunch break, I left the flowers on the table in the house, then found Jerry in his studio.

"Hi baby! Happy Birthday, my love!" I ran over and hugged him.

"Hey, momma. Thank you for love letter, that was awesome," he replied.

"I love you baby. I'm hungry today. Do you want to come inside for a few minutes with me?" I asked.

We turned off his lights and closed up shop, then headed into the house.

"Oh momma, why? You know you didn't have to get me anything. Sarah, they are beautiful, I mean, wow! Oh shit, that's awesome, a square vase. You shouldn't have bought them, but I love them," Jerry said.

"Baby stop. Just this once I wanted to surprise you. You deserve a lot more than just flowers," I said.

"Momma, you're awesome. But a few regular flowers would have been fine. Anything from you is awesome. It's the fact that you thought about me and wanted to get me flowers. Baby, you could have picked weeds from the yard, and I would have loved them."

"I know, but I really wanted to do this."

"Where's my kiss and my hug? Did you forget about that today or something?" Jerry asked.

"Me forget about kissing you? I don't think so."

Our lunch hour was over quickly as they always are, and I headed back to work.

The next month, Jerry and I had our second art show. This time we invested in our own tent, the price being the same as a weekend rental, and Jerry made us new walls to hang our paintings on. We sold fifteen paintings that weekend and he received many compliments. "Excellent work, or Wow, great work," people would say. "Excellent work doesn't pay the bills," Jerry would say as they walked away. I don't think anyone except me heard him, as the people were already out of the tent, but it's not like he has a quiet voice, so you never know. The most fun for me, besides selling his work, was listening to him. We would watch all the different people walk through the festival, and he had a story to tell for each and every one. He had me rolling most of the weekend.

Even with the festival, we were tight for money, so we looked forward to our summer cleaning jobs.

A Soulmates Twin Flame

"I know we have shows coming up to make some money, but that's just one weekend. Maybe we'll get a call in early March this year," Jerry said. We had been struggling to keep bills paid and couldn't afford more canvas.

"Yeah, I hope so. Our so-called summer cleaning is usually for six or seven months each year, and we make great money. I like not having to clip coupons and buying stuff we want, not just what we need."

"But baby, if you still did the coupons, and we looked for sales too, we would have more money. I don't like coupons, but you know I'll help. I like being able to go to work and make money every week. I don't think you understand how good it makes me feel," Jerry said.

"I would switch with you in a heartbeat, and it wouldn't bother me one bit that I wasn't making money because I know the job at home is harder, and you'd pay me very well, and I don't mean monetarily."

"Momma, you're funny, and you're darn right I'd pay you well. We still have to try and make our money last, so we don't struggle so much through the winter months. I can't figure out how we blow through an extra four hundred dollars a week, and then double that when we work both Saturday and Sunday."

"Well, some of it is that I buy whatever I want when food shopping, and don't forget, I make sure you buy extra bags of pot so we don't run out. I have my stash for when you run low, and you have yours. You go through it to fast when you have multiple bags right in front of you, and that shit gets expensive. Between the pot and cigarettes, we spend about eight hundred a month on our smoking habits. Don't say a word, I'm not ready to quit smoking."

"I know you're not. I want to quit, but we need to do it together. When you're ready, we will both try."

"Okay, but you're not giving up your pot. You need that, and I way prefer you smoke over needing prescription drugs. Besides, I'm not sure what I would do without my aromatherapy each night," I said.

Sarah J Provost

"I said cigarettes! You're out of your tree if you think I want to quit smoking pot," he said.

After our long Saturdays, we ate dinner and vegged out together. We enjoyed watching Saturday night fights. If there were no fights, we'd find something to watch or rent a movie. It was a rare occasion when he would paint, and I would do computer work on a Saturday night. That year I bought myself a skimpy summer dress to wear when we got home each weekend. I called it my summer Saturday dress, as it was not something I would wear outside the house. Jerry liked it. He would wear something light, that had very thin material. We played while we watched our fights. After working all day and being sweaty, my lips didn't do much exploring on Jerry's body-only my hands did- but it was more than enough. We kept a blanket very close by, just in case a kid decided to come out of their room. Even though he liked it, I tried to sometimes hold myself back, so he didn't think I was crazy. He showed plenty of affection too, and I loved it, but I was still afraid that he'd think I was insane or simply get tired of me being all over him.

A Soulmates Twin Flame

Fury and Fun

Fighting, laughing, and loving

Isabelle for Christmas last year received two tickets to see Maroon Five in Columbia, South Carolina, but the concert wasn't until September. Concert day had arrived. Jerry and I thought it would be fun to spend the night walking around downtown Columbia while she was at the show.

We dropped Isabelle and her friend off at the venue. Jerry and I walked around for a little while. We looked at a few shops, got a bite to eat and realized that we were in a college area and the only thing to do was sit at a bar and drink. We said no to that. We started driving looking for something to do. Jerry was getting frustrated and bored. We found nothing. Jerry wasn't even in a talking mood anymore as he had become so irritated. We were in front of the concert building and I decided to buy two tickets off a scalper out front. We found our seats and enjoyed the show.

October 2016 and we had to prepare for Hurricane Matthew, and at first, I was excited, just to see a hurricane. But after the first day when we went to the beach to take pictures, I and the other employees worked in twenty-hour shifts, helping to restore power to thousands of people in our area. The long hours were horrible. I missed my husband that night and was trying to stay awake sitting at my desk. He was miserable too, and we texted for a while until he went to bed at about two in the morning.

The storm came a week before our next art show. We got lucky that there was minimal damage to the beaches, and the festival was still a go. Our big weekend was upon us, and I was more excited than the last show. Jerry said that he was now more comfortable showing off his work, and his growing confidence showed. When repeat customers walked into the tent and took down a few paintings to purchase, Jerry was like a kid in a candy shop who couldn't be contained. I handled the credit cards just like last time, and Jerry packaged up their paintings.

"Holy shit, momma, can you believe it? They just bought three more paintings. I remember them from last time. I don't remember what they said their name was, but who cares? They just bought three more paintings," Jerry said.

"I know baby, I know. I told you your paintings are excellent, but you need people to buy them to prove that. That's eight paintings we sold today, and we still have tomorrow," I said.

"Are you kidding me, we sold eight today?" He asked.

"Yes, we sold eight thus far today."

"Sarah, you are amazing. I don't know what I would do without you. If it wasn't for you, we wouldn't be here and you know I sure wasn't going to sit in front of the computer and fill out those forms. You do all this work for me. I love you so much, momma," he said and hugged me.

"Baby, I do it for us. I love you, and I will make our dreams come true. You know that. I have never enjoyed anything like I do this. You create masterpieces, and I get to show them off and take pictures and brag about my husband. It's awesome that we get to do it all together. Less than eight years, baby, and I quit and still get full benefits for us."

"Just wait, momma, before you know it we will be traveling everywhere in our RV doing art shows, and I'll be doing paintings of the different places we go, while you enjoy photographing everything we see. Momma, you need to start doing more with your pictures. People pay good money for scenic prints, and some of your photos are awesome."

A Soulmates Twin Flame

"I know, that's what I want to do when I quit my job. We will have two shops. One for paintings, and the other for photography," I said.

Art Shows, always a blast!

A Soulmates Twin Flame

We sold a few more paintings that day, and a couple on Sunday. In between, we got in hours of people-watching. Once again, Jerry-the-storyteller was quick to put a story to everything he saw and make me laugh my ass off all weekend. He liked to laugh at himself too. The next week at work, I got a message to call him at home.

"Hey momma, how's my girl? You know how much I love you, right? Jerry said in his cute have-pity-on-me tone.

"Yes, what happened, my love? I asked.

"Okay, so as I was getting up to go outside, I bumped the stool where the laptop was sitting and well, it fell, it's broken and I couldn't fix it. Baby, I am so sorry."

"Are you serious?"

"Baby, I am so sorry. I know how much all the photos mean to you."

"All of our photo shoots were on there."

"Momma, you know we can make more anytime. We were going to anyways."

"I know, and we will. I don't want anyone else seeing our pictures. We can just smash it one day. We need another computer if I'm gonna keep our shop going."

We got another computer a week later. A few weeks later, I got another message to call Jerry. He again told me that he broke our new laptop. He was walking into the living room and dropped it. That time I just laughed. I had not put any important pictures on that computer yet. All his painting photos were there, but I was easily able to retake those. A few days after that we got another computer and had a new rule. Jerry was not allowed to remove the laptop from the desk. I came home from work one afternoon and Isabelle couldn't wait to tell me about dad.

"Mom, dad is so funny," Isabelle said

"Why, what did he do this time?" I asked.

"He said he wanted to show me a picture on the computer. I said I was having a snack in the kitchen and to come out and show me. He said he couldn't, so I asked why because it's a laptop. He said he just couldn't, and I said to him that all he had to do was bring it out and show me."

"Dad is not allowed to move the computer from the desk," I said.

"I know, that's what he said! He said, 'That's mom's new rule, and if I break another one she's not going to be happy.' He sounded like a kid the way he was telling me. I couldn't help but laugh, and he listened, mom. Dad followed your rule."

Jerry and I had started looking for a new place to live in December 2016. He had noticed the neighborhood we lived in had been going downhill and thought it was time to get out.

I was home for my lunch hour and couldn't stand the way our house vibrated any longer. I told Jerry that I would talk to the neighbors and ask them to please lower their music. He said he'd do it, but I knew that you get more with sugar than you do vinegar. Jerry only knows vinegar when he's angry about something. I walked next door.

"Excuse me, sir, I am sorry to bother you, but you could please lower your music? We can hear it and feel the vibration from it in our house when all the doors and windows are closed," I said politely.

"Get the fuck away from me, bitch, you don't hear fucking shit. You don't know what the fuck you're talking about. My fucking shit ain't loud. Get the fuck back in your house, bitch. I'd better not see you anywhere near my mother fucking property. I said get the fuck back in your house, bitch!" I stood there with my mouth open, not believing my ears.

A Soulmates Twin Flame

Jerry was furious and tried his best to coax the neighbor into the street. His plan was to get the guy to take a swing at him in front of witnesses so he could hit him back in self-defense. Not only would the neighbor not take the bait, but he let Jerry know he had a weapon that he would use if he had to. That was the day that we decided it was time to move, and the sooner the better.

For Christmas that year, we returned to our no-presents policy. But that didn't mean I couldn't get creative. While he was in the shower on Christmas Eve, I got naked and covered myself in Christmas bows.

"Baby, I know we don't normally give each other Christmas gifts, but I really wanted to give you something," I said.

"Momma, you didn't have to get me anything," he replied.

"I know, but I think you are really going to like it."

"I'm almost done, be out in a minute."

Jerry got out of the shower, and his whole face lit up like a Christmas tree when he saw me waiting for him covered in bows.

"Momma, you are awesome and beautiful. This is the best gift ever, and I had no idea what you were doing out there. Wow, you're amazing!" he said.

"Thank you, baby, I'm glad you like your gift. Why don't you come unwrap your gift so I can take a shower," I said.

"My pleasure, my love. I can't wait to play with my Christmas gift tonight," he said.

Jerry took every bow off my body with a huge smile, and I received the most wonderful kiss. He grabbed a large bag and put every bow in a bag and labeled it 'my Christmas gift 2016'. After many years he realized that I was not someone who wanted anything bought at a store. His affection and love letters from his heart brought me to a level of happiness that you could never get with money. "There has to be at least one thing you want," Jerry would say to me around holiday times. And I would just say, "Yes, and that is you."

A few days after Christmas, we found a new house to rent. It was a little smaller and more expensive, but I told Jerry I would figure it out. Jerry said he really liked the location, as did I. He said he felt his family would be safe in this new area, and he no longer had to worry.

We packed up our house very quickly, as we had signed a lease that allowed us to move in on January 1st, 2017. While we were packing, we took a break because it was New Year's Eve, time for the Provost family tradition. The four of us played Monopoly that night, taking a break halfway through to make snacks. Then we played Scategories and the fun went to frustration. We were trying to think of vegetables that started with a "B".

"Ok what did you guys get for a vegetable?" I asked.

"Blue Potatoes. I was going to put broccoli, but I thought at least one you would have had that written down, so I had to think of something different," replied Jerry. The rest of us had written nothing on our cards.

"Baby, there is no such thing as blue potatoes. Wow, I can't believe none of us thought of broccoli," I said.

"Yes, there is."

"I have never heard of blue potatoes. Where can we buy them?" I asked.

"You can't buy them anywhere."

"Exactly, then it doesn't count, because there is no such thing."

"Ah, but there is such a thing."

"What?" I asked.

"C'mon, momma, don't you remember. It was a special I created at work, and the garnish was decorated blue potatoes."

"Yes, I remember, but you made them blue."

"They were blue potatoes, weren't they? It's not my fault you guys lack imagination. I get a point for blue potatoes," he said.

"Seriously?" asked Isabelle.

"No, I said it because it makes me feel all warm and fuzzy inside," said Jerry, grinning like a fool.

"Okay, fine you get a point for your blue potatoes," I said.

By the time we finished the games, it was time to watch the ball drop and ring in the New Year. 2017 was going to be a fantastic year. I could just feel it.

Even stronger and older

A Soulmates Twin Flame

When a House is a Home

Love is bold

By the time we moved in our new house, a studio for Jerry was a must. Our bedroom was easily half the house, so we turned part of it into his studio. Another must, was a large tub for the two of us, which this house had. Neither of us could live without tub time, especially in the winter. In the summer months, there were a few times we turned the air conditioner lower and made the house cold just so we could get into a warm bath together.

Jerry and I did what some people would call crazy or silly, but for us it was fun. We got tired of the bed being so cold in the winter, so after my shower, I would blow dry my hair, then I would blow dry Jerry. We would both go into the bedroom and I would blow dry the bed. It took about five minutes to get it nice and toasty warm. The entire time he would stand and watch me, and he always had something to say.

"That is one fine ass you got baby. Wow, you are so fucking sexy." We would get into bed and soak up all the warmth, and then I would get into my "parking spot."

I was blow drying Jerry one night after a shower.

"Alright baby, you have to let me know if it gets too hot but I have to blow dry your backside better, and make sure the hair is dry on your ass," I said while laughing.

"Yeah, yeah go ahead, keep laughing," he replied.

"Is it too hot?" I asked.

"It gets a little hot when you don't move it enough. You know I was thinking about trimming back there too, but I can't see like I can the front."

"I'll trim back there for you. Grab me the clippers and then you can take another shower."

"Okay, thanks. I trust you momma, but still be careful, it's a little scary handing you a pair of clippers and me not being able to see what you're doing."

"Don't worry, just bend over and spread 'em," I said.

I trimmed all the hair and had him spread his cheeks as wide as possible, and I went to work shaving as much as possible, then Jerry got back into the shower.

"Holy shit, this is awesome. If you stop and think about it, how clean have I really been? I feel so much cleaner now. That's why the bidet was invented. It was for men, to clean the hair on their asses after sitting on the toilet. Baby, thank you, you're awesome my love," Jerry said while he was in the shower and I was cleaning up.

As evening set each day, I couldn't wait for our time. No matter what the day brought, seeing his face and knowing that in a few hours we were going to close off the world after we said goodnight to the kids was what I looked forward to every day. Some days were harder than others to wait until it was bedtime, especially when the playfulness together was nonstop.

It had been quite some time since we pulled out a toy to add to our evenings. I asked Jerry one night about toys and he said he preferred just our bodies. That was all I wanted, but I thought that Jerry would get bored.

"I only want you, baby," he said. "All we need are hands and lips and the love we have for each other."

A Soulmates Twin Flame

I snuggled up to him in agreement. After all these years together, I was still at a loss for words and let Jerry do most of the talking. When I tried to explain exactly what I felt and wanted I would stumble over my words to the point that Jerry would laugh and say, "Baby, just stop, I get it." It was a problem I'd had since childhood, but with Jerry, I expressed myself through touch. Jerry always expressed his appreciation.

"Sarah, thank you for loving me so much in the way that you do," Jerry said one evening.

"You're welcome, my love. Loving you is the easiest thing I have done in my life," I replied.

I came from work one afternoon, and Jerry told me that he had done a few things in the bedroom. He had wrapped our red rope light around a pole and hung it across the ceiling over our bed. He said he wanted to see my body glow in the red light at night instead of the plain white light from our lamp.

"Oh, I love it!" I said. But of course, I would. I loved everything about Jerry, even his smell. I sniffed the air by his mouth.

"Okay baby, I think I smell cherry. Am I right?" I asked. Jerry had a habit of sucking hard candies.

"You're good, momma. It's cherry," he replied. "Want some?" We kissed, and Jerry slipped the sticky candy into my mouth with his tongue.

In a few minutes, he wanted it back, so we kissed again and I returned the little sliver of cherry to his mouth.

"You guys are so gross, that's disgusting," I heard from the hallway. It was Isabelle. "Can you just not do that when we're around? Ulllkkkk." She made a sound like she was gagging. Jerry and I fell on the bed, laughing.

Super Bowl Sunday in our new house brought us together as a family. In past years, the kids would trail off after halftime and snacks, but this year, the

Sarah J Provost

Patriots were playing, and we were all fans. It was a cliffhanger of a game, and by the time our team pulled off an amazing win in the final minutes of the game, we were all on our feet, cheering them on and hugging one another.

"Mark this date on the calendar," Jerry said. "It's the first time that the four of us have ever watched an entire Super Bowl game together."

It was indeed a memorable day. Already our new house was a home.

A Soulmates Twin Flame

The Fairytale

Sunshine and Rainbows

Building on our success at art festivals, we applied for a bigger venue in the spring, an art show in Wilmington, North Carolina. Jerry had heard from other artists that it was a tough show to get into and he fretted about it while we waited to hear back on the application we had submitted.

"There have only been a handful of things I've been certain about in my life, and one of them is your art. I wish you would believe in yourself as much as I do," I told him.

Even after we were accepted, he worried. Just a few days before the show, he had a premonition.

"I just have a feeling something is going to go wrong, he said.

"Would you just stop? You're so negative. Even if something does go wrong, we'll find a way to work through it."

"Okay, honey. I do love your positive outlook on everything. I'm trying to follow your never-ending light, but I don't see it like you do."

When we arrived to set up, it was already quite windy. We unpacked the car and had everything on the sidewalk as the wind seemed to be getting stronger. I checked the weather on the phone and there were wind warnings issued, but no storms. The forecast read sustained winds at twenty-five to thirty-five miles per hour, and gusts that could exceed fifty miles per hour.

"I think it's a typo; let's start trying to set up," I said. The winds very soon became ridiculous and impossible to work in. We tried multiple times to at least get the tent up, but it was not happening. Jerry was so frustrated and swearing at everything. He said he was done and we were going home.

"No, we are not done, and we are not going home. You can get pissed and yell at me all you want, but we are not leaving," I said.

Jerry didn't say a word to me after that. I knew if anyone could figure out a solution, it would be him. He just needed to calm down for a few minutes. The silence ended after five minutes, and he said he had an idea. With a new plan in place, we got our tent set up and gave one another a high five.

We sold our first painting that evening while still hanging them on the wall. Jerry was in awe.

"I told you, stop doubting yourself so much." I then got my well-deserved kiss and hug.

We had a magnificent weekend, exceeding sales from previous shows, and Jerry said over and over that it was awesome. This event was such a great boost for our spirits in the art world and exactly what Jerry needed to help build his confidence.

Just two weeks later and we attended the local beach festival. It was a great weekend, full of smiles and laughter. We saw repeat customers and new customers who loved his work. At the end of the weekend, I looked at him and said,

"Baby, it looks to me like our dreams are finally starting to take shape. I knew they would, I just didn't know when."

"I know, this is fucking awesome. I can't believe it. It's still all thanks to you, my love. You found a way to make all this happen for us. Wow, I love you Sarah, and I certainly know how much you love me," he said.

Finally, we could daydream together about what our future could look like and the places we would travel to for art events. We talked about how much we

A Soulmates Twin Flame

enjoyed doing everything together and being partners in the whole art business we were building. I reminded him that I only had so many years left at my job before and it was full-time art for both of us. Jerry smiled and threw his arms around me. I sucked up every ounce of affection from him.

Azalea Festival   April 2017
Wilmington, North Carolina

A Soulmates Twin Flame

My birthday arrived, and Jerry bought me a gift. Other than his flowers last year, it had been over a decade since we bought each other birthday presents. I received a singing teddy bear and attached to its hat were a pair of earrings. The best part of the gift, though, was a handwritten love letter.

Later in the spring, Isabelle decided that she wanted a dog, and Jerry thought it was a great idea. I wanted nothing to do with it. We already had two cats, but the dog lovers in the family won and agreed to take full responsibility for its care. Into our family came Mollie, a two-year-old black lab that Jerry adopted from the animal shelter.

She was a pain in the ass. She whined all day anytime she saw or heard anything. Every bird that flew by the window had to be investigated. Jerry got so frustrated.

"I don't know if I can take this every day, but I am trying. Every time I sit down to paint, I get two minutes and Mollie is whining again to go outside because of a fucking bird," he said.

"It's only been a week, let's take her back. I didn't want a dog anyways," I replied.

"The kids love her. Are you going to break it to them? It's just gonna take some time to train her. I know you don't want her outside unless she on a leash to go to the bathroom, because you think the house is going to smell if she gets dirty."

"It will smell like fucking dog, and I don't want a house that smells like dog. It's gross, let's just bring her back to the shelter."

"No, I will train her. She will learn. I like having a dog. She's gonna protect my three."

"Whatever. I will help check why she's whimpering in the evenings and walk her so you can get a little painting time in." It was the last thing I wanted to do, but—as usual—I couldn't resist offering my help to Jerry.

"Thank you, momma. I love my circle of four."

It took another month, but Mollie finally got used to her new home and calmed down with the non-stop whimpering. Jerry and Mollie were playing one afternoon when I walked in the door from work.

"Hey baby, I missed you. It's about time your home," Jerry said.

"I missed you too! What are you doing?" I asked.

"Playing with Mollie. You know I never thought this would happen, but someone has you beat for affection. She is all over me like white on rice. She cries now because I'm not petting her and sitting with her. The last few days, she stares at me while I am trying to paint, and after a few minutes will make weird noises until I pet her or sit on the floor with her. She follows me everywhere."

"I don't know what to tell you on that one. I doubt she's got me beat for affection though. At least I don't whine about it. I mean, sometimes I do stare at you, but that's because my husband is sexy."

"Yeah, ok, sexy. You might want to get a second opinion on your so-called perfect vision, honey," he replied.

"Been there, done that. Still have perfect vision. Don't go anywhere I want to get some pictures of Mollie." I said.

"Whatever you say dear,"

I Grabbed the camera and spent a few minutes taking pictures of everyone. Even got some great surprise photos of the kids.

20 Years of surprises

A Soulmates Twin Flame

Summer Saturdays as the Jerry/Sarah cleaning crew were back in full swing. We were driving around the beach one morning and I grabbed a pen to make some notes about the house we had just finished cleaning. I saw a piece of paper that was folded and my name written on it. I dropped the pen and immediately began to read it.

Dear Sarah,

> *It has been a couple of years that we have been together and I find myself at a loss for words. I'm looking and looking for 17 years of marriage of a better and more clever way to express my level of love. Nothing expresses the way my heart melts or starts to beat a little faster when you enter the room. Twenty years and I still get butterflies in my stomach. So, thank you for teaching me what love is and how it feels. I love you.*

"Thank you for my love letter," I said to Jerry when we got home.

"You're blind; its been there for days now," he said.

The day had arrived for us to celebrate that our little girl was graduating high school. How quickly she had grown up! Isabelle had received early graduation honors and finished school in January, so the last five months had been at home with dad. Jerry and Isabelle had fought a lot over the years, but these months had brought them closer. Jerry taught her how to drive during this time, and they had hours of time talking and laughing together. Isabelle said that she and her dad were just alike, and I agreed.

Jerry's mother flew down to see Isabelle graduate. Jerry picked his mom up from the airport and was there when I dropped Brendan at home during my lunch hour. By the time I came home from work that evening, the mood had changed, and I felt that Jerry was giving me the cold shoulder. We went to bed together but something was missing. Had he argued with his mom? Did she give him some bad news he didn't want to discuss? I only knew that something was off.

"Snuggle with me, baby," I said to him finally.

He did not and instead, got up and stood at the end of the bed. I turned the lamp back on and looked at him. He didn't look angry. He had a look of sadness and confusion.

"You don't have to take off your makeup anymore when you come home for lunch because I won't be here any longer," Jerry said calmly.

"What? What are you talking about, my love?" I asked.

"You heard me, don't worry about taking off your makeup when you come to see me at lunch and pretend this is where you want to be. I saw you today. I saw where you missed a spot cleaning your face. I saw the makeup on you, and I won't be here anymore," he explained. Was he fucking crazy?

"Okay, I am very confused right now," I said

"Confused about what? It's simple. You don't have to go through the trouble of pretending you want to be with me. I'm leaving."

"Are you kidding me? You know I brought Isabelle to work today, and when I hugged her and her cheek touched mine, I wouldn't doubt a little makeup rubbed off on me with how much she cakes it on. I don't even own makeup, you know this. I don't understand you sometimes. If I saw something on you that looked like it could be lipstick, I'd laugh and point it out to you and ask about it, because for all I know, it could be paint. I wouldn't just assume you were cheating on me with another woman. You could have easily asked me about it or spent a minute thinking and remember that I brought our daughter to work today and she always hugs her mother. It's that simple. I am having a hard time understanding how you create these crazy stories."

"That's how my mind works. Sarah, I'm sorry, I know you don't own makeup or wear any. I wasn't thinking, and I was wrong, but you don't seem to understand how bad my mind can get with these thoughts. Maybe you need to grow a thicker skin."

"That's not the problem. The problem is when the story is about me, it's always me leaving you, cheating on you or something of that nature. Why can't your story about me be fun, or romantic, or anything like that? That's what I don't understand, Jerry."

"You're right and I don't understand why mind works this way. Maybe I need help, but you still need to grow thicker skin."

"Jerry, I love you. I will never leave you; you are my world."

"I know, you need to try and get some sleep. You have work in the morning."

"I'm gonna step outside for a minute. When I come back in, will you come and snuggle with me?"

"Always. Sarah, I'm sorry, I didn't mean to upset you."

I went outside for a smoke and to think. I was baffled by his story. It had been at least ten years since I had worn makeup. It had been a few years since either of us expressed fears of losing the other one. What drove these insecurities in Jerry? I went back in the house. We snuggled for a few minutes and he held me while I fell asleep.

Graduation day was long, and that evening, Jerry's mom wanted to take us all out to dinner to celebrate. Jerry wasn't feeling good and said he didn't want to go. I was disappointed.

"Jerry told me you need to start doing things without him," his mom told me at dinner.

But we enjoyed doing everything together. Errands, yardwork, a ride down the street—Jerry always wanted me at his side. I kept my thoughts to myself because it made no sense. None at all.

I was on the computer one morning, and Jerry said he wanted to talk to me about something.

"Hey momma, you need to look at mother's rings. I know I wanted to buy you a new engagement ring, but I really feel like you need a new mothers ring. The one you wear now has only Isabelle's birthstone. You need one that shows both kids," Jerry said.

"I don't want a mother's ring, I don't need one. Look baby, I found a couple's ring, that's what I want, or we can pick out a new engagement ring together," I replied.

"No, you need a mother's ring. I want you to have it. You have two children and need a new one."

"I don't understand why. I like the engagement ring idea better. We already talked about it, and there's no way we can do both."

"No, you deserve a mother's ring. Pick one out, please, or I'll do it myself, and you might not like it."

I picked out a mother's ring and showed Jerry. He loved it and ordered it right away. It was pretty, but I still had my heart set on a new engagement ring. Jerry and I had talked many times about celebrating our twentieth wedding anniversary by renewing our wedding vows. This time we wanted to write our own. The kids were excited too about their mom and dad getting remarried.

Mother's Day, then Father's Day came. There were presents from the kids, breakfast in bed for me, a night off from cooking for him. As always, we exchanged letters. Jerry took his one step further and created a piece of framed art for me about being a mother. The picture he drew was beautiful and carried so much symbolism. The art was also a letter and read:

> *It's hard to explain how awesome it is to watch the makings of a good mother. Like the universe we can't explain how it all keeps us here, but a mother knows, and a mother's love is out of this world. Happy Mother's Day!*

"You're an amazing woman," Jerry told me. "Women are gifts from God because of their beauty and the way only a woman can create a new life on this earth," he said.

"Women are awesome, but it takes a male to actually create a life," I replied. Jerry gave me an odd look. "It's true! If it wasn't for you, I couldn't have given life to our children."

We saw life from different angles, me and Jerry. I had a hard time remembering my life without Jerry in it. There had been a few nights over the last year where we'd be in bed snuggling and Jerry would say, "I just want to hold you tonight. I am so in love with you, and I just want you in my arms and the feel of your body against mine like we are now, and never let go. We fell asleep that way a few times. One night I looked into Jerry's eyes, and we both chuckled. We knew what the other was thinking, and I said, "Who would have thought, over twenty years now, and the feelings still keep growing. This is incredible." He looked at me and said, "I know baby, fucking intense. Sarah, I love you."

As silly as it sounded to other people, our life together was pink hearts, unicorns and rainbows. We lived in a fairytale, most of the time.

Sarah J Provost

We had a welcome surprise in July when my brother and his family came to visit. They were several hours into the drive when we heard they had rented a nearby house on the beach and were on their way! It had been three years since we had seen them, so a fun visit at the beach was long overdue. Jerry was delighted to see them too, and we enjoyed catching up with one another. When the week was over it was back to focusing on a few upcoming art events.

Still enjoying the beach

Sarah J Provost

Jerry was working on a large piece that was going to be displayed in an art gallery for six months. I was so proud of how far he had come with his art, and I could see his confidence growing, along with our dreams. I was photographing some of his artwork and struggling with location and lighting. I didn't say anything to him about it, but he saw how I kept moving things from outside to inside and to different rooms, trying to find the perfect spot. I came home one day, and he showed me my new photography area that he had designed himself. His creativity was never-ending. I loved it, and the lighting worked perfectly; my photos looked exactly like the paintings, and the colors were not off. Jerry always paid attention whether I said something or not.

We didn't work on art every night. Some nights we would rent a movie. Other times Jerry would say grab your camera, we're going for a ride. We would go to the beach, and I would get beautiful pictures of the sunsets or the waves, or anything for that matter. Jerry was my favorite photography subject, and nature of any kind came in second place.

We were getting ready for work one Saturday morning and Jerry was loading the car with all our supplies.

"Hey, momma, grab your camera, quick. Hurry and come outside. You're going to love this," he yelled from the doorway.

"Okay, what is it?" I asked, getting the camera.

"Look directly above you at the sky."

"Oh my God, Jerry, that is beautiful, wow!"

"I know, right? When was the last time you saw a double rainbow?"

"I don't know if I have ever seen a double rainbow, just pictures."

I took many photos of the double rainbow that morning. After that, Jerry and I stood, holding hands, just looking at the sky, until he said we had to get going or we'd be late.

I'm serious, you should really concentrate on your photography more," Jerry said in the car.

"I will, when I quit my job."

"Your photos can go up in our online store," he said. "They're both arts, and they will attract more people."

"All in good time, honey," I told him.

My favorite photography subject

A Soulmates Twin Flame

August had arrived quickly and things felt like they were all falling into place. Jerry and I would flip the switch from mom and dad to Jerry and Sarah a little earlier in the evenings. We'd say goodnight to the kids and tell them mom and dad are going to bed. We would get a sarcastic *ok* from both of them.

Jerry and I had finally bought ourselves a tv for the bedroom. We would turn on the jazz or classical music channel while taking our showers. Every once in a while, I would turn on some rock, until it was time to lie down, and we'd change the channel back to something similar to classical. Once in bed, we'd talk for a few minutes, and he would ask me to get into my "parking spot."

While talking in bed one night, we had discussed doing another photo shoot. Jerry had an idea to cover the bedroom with plastic sheeting and pour different colors of paints all over the floor. We would play together, rolling around in our paint, and let the camera catch all of our moments together. We added it to the 'gonna do real soon' list.

Lying there, content, in my parking spot, I had an overwhelming feeling that I needed to verbalize my feelings to Jerry. I looked into his eyes and said, "You will always be the only man for me. I am so in love with you. There will never be anyone else." On this night, I didn't think my body language said enough. Jerry knew that verbalizing my feelings wasn't easy for me unless he had initiated it. I saw tears in his eyes.

His arms held onto me a little tighter after that.

I walked in the door one afternoon at lunch and Jerry said, "Hey, Sarah." I just said, "Hi, baby." This continued for a few more days where every time he said something to me, he used my name. I had to ask because it made feel somewhat uncomfortable.

"Baby, this seems really awkward to me. Why have you been using my name so much? You never do that. You always call me either momma, baby, or my love. What is up?" I asked.

Sarah J Provost

"I just want to hear you say my name more," he said.

"Okay, fine Jerry."

I tried to remember that he wanted to hear his name more, but he was my baby and my love and that's what I called him most of the time.

Jerry had been putting the finishing touches on his painting for the art gallery, and we argued about me submitting his work to a nationwide juried art contest. He said it was a waste because he wasn't going to win. I said he was crazy and did it anyway. The theme was seascapes, and I uploaded five of Jerry's paintings-the max I was allowed to show, or I would have entered all his work.

The kids were now eighteen and thirteen and didn't join us on many family outings because we were—quite frankly—boring! I had requested Monday, August 21st, off from work so Jerry and I could drive a little further south and watch the solar eclipse. Totality was to occur only forty-five minutes from our house. We asked the kids if they wanted to go with us and, to our surprise, they both said yes.

We got up that morning and hoped the weather forecasters were wrong, but they weren't. It was cloudy and supposed to rain all day. We told the kids we were still going to take a ride and hope for a break in the weather. We had lunch together and hoped for a break in the clouds, but our wishes got us nowhere. The weather didn't change and we didn't see anything. Still, we had a good time, the four of us, and there was no complaining from anyone which was rare.

We got back home, and Jerry and I took Mollie out for a walk. He told me how bad he felt that we didn't get to see the eclipse, knowing that I was excited. I said it was ok, that I still had a good time with the four us talking, laughing and having lunch together. Jerry was excited as the day turned into evening.

"Hey, momma, guess what?"

A Soulmates Twin Flame

"What?" I asked

"So, I found out that there is another total eclipse coming where totality will be in the United States," he said.

"Really, where?"

"Totality will be in Illinois, and we are going, baby. It will be just the two of us by then, back to Sarah and Jerry."

"I can't wait. We can get a hotel for a few days and explore Illinois. That would be fun, just the two of us."

"I know momma, we are raising wonderful children, but soon, my love, it will be our adventure time together again."

"I have been waiting a long time for just the two of us again. I love our babies, and maybe we will visit grandchildren in our future, but Jerry, I really can't wait until it's just us again. I'm excited!"

Jerry and I were making a simple dinner one night after the almost-eclipse.

"Hey baby, can you please help me open this?" I asked.

"Alright, I want to show you something. What would you do if I wasn't here?"

"Would you just knock it off, and please open the jar."

"No, really, watch I'm gonna show you an easy trick to open it."

"Fine, thank you for helping me. I love you, baby."

We made dinner watched tv and headed to bed for our nightly "fireworks." In the last few months, the explosions were incredible. The Jerry and Sarah fireworks had grown bigger, brighter, and louder.

Jerry making our dreams a reality

A Soulmates Twin Flame

The Unknown

Love knows no boundaries

Thursday, August 31st, 2017, started like any other day. I dropped Brendan at school and went to work. Mid-morning, I got a text from Jerry. All it read was, *Sarah*. I replied back, *Jerry*. I quickly sent him another message asking if he was ok. Six minutes later, I received a reply back: *No*. I sent him another message that read *Be home soon for lunch to radiate my love and good feelings. Also, its payday trying calling someone else for a bag.* He was out of marijuana for a few days and was totally miserable and not feeling good. I didn't receive anything back and went outside to send a message in case we were dealing with bad reception in my office. I sent another message. Ten more minutes went by and I had a nauseating feeling in my stomach. I texted my daughter and asked her to go check on her father immediately. Five minutes went by without a word. I left work and ran to the car while I called her. She answered the phone crying, and I asked her if daddy was alive. She said no. A paramedic took her phone while I was screaming and said to me, "Ma'am your husband is deceased."

I finally got to the house and there were so many people there. I ran inside, saw Isabelle with a police officer and went right into the bedroom. I laid on the floor next to Jerry and told him how much I loved him. I took his glasses off, kissed him, held him in my arms and rested my face against his until I was forced to leave.

Isabelle said that as she got close to the bedroom, she saw her father on the floor, called 911 and started CPR on her dad. An ambulance was there in less than five minutes, but they could not get a pulse. I had my mother go to the school to pick up Brendan.

Sarah J Provost

We waited outside for what seemed like forever and were not allowed in the house until the medical examiner arrived. I did my best to comfort Isabelle and tell her there was nothing she could do and not blame herself. I knew my husband had passed almost an hour before she found him. I had a weird feeling right after I received the *No* message but didn't understand it. I saw the phone on the floor when I first arrived and saw that the first message I sent about a bag was unread. I can only hope that Jerry did not suffer and his pain was minimal.

It was about two hours later that we were allowed back in. Jerry was now lying on a stretcher and covered with a blanket. I brought Brendan in to say goodbye to his daddy. He looked at his father and fell to the ground crying; he stood back up, looked at Jerry, said goodbye and left the room. I stayed with him until I was again told I had to leave. I kissed his cheek, held his hand and again told him that I loved him and needed him.

Then I said, "You love me, and you know how much I love you. You would never leave me. This body is just a shell, and you are still here, right by my side and always will be."

They brought Jerry out to the transport vehicle and told us that an autopsy would be done because he was so young and had no prior health issues. The house was flooded with people, some I knew, and others I didn't. Regardless, I didn't see anyone. I felt so empty and alone. All I wanted was Jerry back or for God to take me home too. I had to be there for the kids, but the pain was so intense and shot through every part of my body. I couldn't grasp the fact that I would never see his face again, hear his voice, see his beautiful smile. I would never get to hold him or feel his arms around me ever again. It was all I could do to breathe, and I was really hoping the breathing would just come to an end.

I talked to Jerry's mom that night and explained to her that I didn't understand how something like this could happen to us. We always knew when something was wrong and had a feeling. Why did my sick feeling and the knowing that he was gone come an hour too late? I wanted to know why. I should have been there with him. If I couldn't save him, then I would have at least been there with him, and he wouldn't have been alone. Her words to me were,

"Sarah, I know your love, God was protecting you. You need to be here for the kids. Do you honestly think that if you watched Jerry take his last breath in your arms, that you would still be here right now? I know you, and I do believe it would have been your last breath as well."

His mom also told me about when Jerry drove her back to the airport to go home in June. He cried, hugged her and said goodbye to her. She said it caught her off-guard because Jerry never used the words goodbye and never cried. He usually waved to her and said, *see you soon*. She said it was odd but didn't think anything of it.

Never did I think anything like this could happen. Jerry was only 46 and had so much life to live and love to give. We had so many plans and plans for a beautiful future together. Jerry's art was finally taking off.

I lost my life that day, my will to live. One second I was on cloud nine, and the next everything was shattered into a million pieces. I was expected to just smile, carry on and raise my children. I died that morning with Jerry, but my body chose to continue living. Jerry and I were passionate soul mates who lived for each other. I always told Jerry that I loved him more than life itself.

Did Jerry have a premonition about leaving us the same way he saw who our children would be before they were born? Just that week he had started online painting classes and was full of joy about everything he was learning. A color wheel he ordered came in the day before, and he had begun a new sketch that he wanted to paint.

Were all the small weird incidences that had happened over the previous three months God's way of trying to prepare us for what was to come? I think

Sarah J Provost

about the mother's ring, the way he wanted to hear his name, showing me how to open a jar, saying that I needed to learn how to do things without him, and the word he chose to use for the first time ever when his mother was flying back home. *Goodbye.*

A Soulmates Twin Flame

Together with Family
With great love comes great pain

We had Jerry flown up to Massachusetts for the wake and funeral. There were many people there, and most I did not know. I recognized some family and a few friends. One person I spoke with was a longtime friend of Jerry's. He said to me that it was amazing how we were so obsessed with each other after that many years together.

I never gave obsession much thought before when it came to our relationship, but he was right. Some say we were crazy for devoting all our time to one another, for forgetting about the friends we had, and shutting out everyone for all those years. I never saw it that way. I was happy, at least most days, and completely in love. I always thought we would have each other through everything, and we would leave this world together. I was wrong.

After the wake, the kids and I stayed with his mom. The funeral was early the next morning. Against the priest's advice, I gave the eulogy for Jerry. No one knew Jerry like I did. No one loved him like me. I did my best, but words— never my strong suit— were not enough to describe my husband.

No one thinks they will leave this world so young, without any notice. The emptiness I feel every day is unbearable. I found a man that I knew was my other half and I was certain I could spend the rest of my life by his side. The pain from this is not something that words could describe. As Jerry always said to me, "Baby, there are no words that could ever truly describe our love." I have experienced things in my life that were painful, including the loss of my father at such a young age, but that pain does not come close or could ever compare to this.

Sarah J Provost

Jerry and I knew our fears. We both feared losing the other one. My worst fear had become a reality. Because of how I chose to live my life with my husband, he is now my support through this. I have made it this far with his help, my children and my beliefs. Jerry knows I need him, and he knew I would be forced to take this journey alone with minimal human connections to lean on. I believe that's why it hit me like a slap in the face when I was saying goodbye. I said goodbye to his physical body, not our love, our bond, and our connection. I have been shown that love is the only force that crosses all realms.

Jerry loved life. He did a colorful painting and all it said was "Love Life". I believe the purpose in life is to discover that unconditional passionate love, and the magic that is created within that love. It's our deep love that keeps us connected and helps me tackle each and every day.

I want to tell the world to cherish love, don't be afraid to love, and cherish every moment with those whom you love. As I have learned, anything can happen at any given moment. Jerry and I never went to bed angry. If we were arguing about something then we resolved it before sleeping, even if that meant being awake for a few days. I could only imagine how I would feel if we went to sleep angry the night before. Jerry was in bed when I left that morning, but I was so fortunate to tell him that I loved him, to kiss him and see his smile before I walked out the door.

What I feel every day is awful, and I have days where the pain makes me physically sick, but I wouldn't trade it. Through great love comes great pain. I loved more than I ever thought possible, and nothing compares to those feelings. I would never trade or give back our life together in order not to experience this. I still believe that Jerry was my gift from God.

The day after Jerry passed, I found out that he won second place in the nationwide art competition I entered him into. It was a bittersweet honor. I received his certificate and framed it. Unfortunately, I had to turn down the interview, and the inclusion to the gallery because they needed the artist. A few months later, Jerry was contacted by a gallery in New York. I was furious. He should be here to celebrate these milestones that we worked so hard to achieve.

There is a saying that time heals all wounds. Not all wounds heal no matter how much time you give it.

Jerry's Paintings

Sarah J Provost

I was in my bathroom one night and saw our two broken laptops on a storage shelf. I was so glad that Jerry and I never got around to smashing them. I brought them to the computer repair shop, and they were able to retrieve ninety-five percent of my photos. It no longer matters to me who sees them, I do not care as long as I get my photos back.

During the first few months of this nightmare, I spent so much time researching everything I could about the heart and how or why his heart failed him. The first night on my own I was walking the dog, and I stopped in my tracks. I felt like I was standing in water, was hit by a wave, and it all came to me about what happened that morning and the week prior.

Jerry and I were at work Saturday morning, and he said he had really bad heartburn. He was sweating and needed to sit for a minute. I was by his side and said to him we should leave and go see a doctor. He said no, that it was just bad heartburn. He had dealt with bad cases of heartburn in the past, and I assumed that this felt the same to him. Ten minutes later he said he felt fine except he felt like his chest was bruised, and he got back to work. We should still go see a doctor, I told him, and he repeated that he was fine. It was a heart attack that he had that morning, and we did not get him help. Little did we know that not treating a heart attack caused an abnormal rhythm, and less than a week later he went into cardiac arrest.

I know I can't blame my myself or him for not seeking treatment, but it's not easy knowing that if we sought treatment that day, he could still be here with me. I forced or pleaded with Jerry to see a doctor for any little ailment and he always listened. Why not this time? Why didn't he think to seek treatment on his own? I try not to think of these things, as I cannot change the past, but sometimes I am haunted by these thoughts.

A Soulmates Twin Flame

All the Days of my Life

Love, a force that can cross any dimension

A friend I saw after the funeral told me that Jerry and I were different from anyone she ever knew. She said we had a relationship that was very different from what she had ever known, almost the reverse from what most people experience. *You should write about it*, she suggested. I dismissed the idea immediately.

Jerry's mom called me one day a month later and said it came to her while she was in church that she needed to tell me to write about our life together. I am not a writer, I told her and once more set aside the idea.

A few days later I had a dream that was very realistic, a visit from Jerry. It was short and brief. We were together, and I was sitting on his lap; he had his arm around me.

I said to him, "I don't want to let you go."

"You have to," he said. "And you need to tell the world about our love. We have something that is so rare, and I see it now. Don't let our love die, tell the world."

I woke up crying. I felt as though he was right next to me even though it was only for the few minutes.

I sat on my back deck talking to Jerry as I do every day and said to him, "Okay, I guess I will write a book." Shortly after that I walked into the house and pulled the phone out of my pocket to call his mom. There was a feather tucked under the case and only a small piece was sticking out. I didn't know what it was at first until I pulled it out and saw a beautiful, large undamaged feather. I have never seen stray feathers outside and we don't have anything in the house that has feathers. I knew instantly that it was a sign from Jerry that I was on the right track with writing. We both always said we were from Missouri, the show-me state. He knew that to leave me a feather in the phone case would eliminate doubt.

When I started writing our story, I thought I was done at forty pages. I then started to get a memory every day from out of the blue. I would make a voice recording so I wouldn't forget and add it to our story. Sometimes I'd say to myself, *that is hilarious, I can't believe I forget about that*. As I would write, all the details from that memory would come flooding back.

I went to see a medium, and Jerry was with me. He said it's not me writing the book, that we were writing it together. I knew that deep down, but still wanted confirmation. I had always been horrible with words. I would labor over a description on Jerry's page for a painting, and all I would come up with was, 'canvas painting, ocean seascape' then I would draw a blank, and he would always come over and tell me the words to type. Now, I write, and the words flow from my fingers with ease.

Never before in my life did I think about life after death or anything spiritual. Everything I experienced was new, unexplored territory. Seeing a medium didn't enter my mind until I talked to Jerry's mom. She called me one morning to tell me she'd had a visit from Jerry.

"All he said was, 'tell Sarah to watch the movie Ghost.'"

I didn't understand why as I had seen the movie a few times already, but I rented it and watched it again. We all know that Whoopie Goldberg can talk to ghosts in the movie. It was the first time she heard Sam that sent a rush of chills through my body and I said, "Oh my God, I need to call a medium." I found someone who was not very far away and made an appointment. She did not ask me for any info, and I called from someone else's phone. I walked in and was given undeniable proof that could only come from Jerry. I felt like I finally found the help I needed.

When I first arrived to see her, I was friendly and had a smile, a fake smile, but nonetheless it was a smile. She said there were two women with me and said one seemed to be a grandmother.

"Now there bringing in a man and he's yelling. He's yelling and saying stop, stop, stop what you're doing. Stop everything that you are doing," she said to me.

"That sounds like who I am here to talk to," I replied

"He keeps going on and on about you needing to stop what you're doing and you are stronger than you give yourself credit for. He's making reference to a friend, he's making me feel like this friend took his own life. He's showing me ninety-five, something with a nine and a five."

Jerry continued to ramble on about me stopping everything I was doing or was trying to do. When Jerry had to leave our session, her final words to me from him were:

"Ok, this is weird. He's saying it's quiet, its finally quiet. Most spirits I communicate with just tell me it's peaceful where they are. He's also pointing to his head and showing me something like misfires, he's saying he had misfires in his head."

Everything she said blew me away. I had spent so much time looking up ways to commit suicide, in-between trying to understand everything about the heart. Every day was a medical journey on how I could sabotage my body and just end this nightmare. Jerry had a friend who was devastated by a loss and committed suicide in 1995. Her final words to me was when I couldn't hold back anymore and began to cry. I wanted to be with him, but I had this brief moment of happiness when he said it was finally quiet. Jerry had complained so many times about his voices and he always said that he wished they would just be quiet.

I see her every month, and every time, I leave knowing I spent an hour communicating with Jerry. He has shared some things with her that I was surprised he'd share and were quite personal, but nonetheless, it proved he was with me.

I know my husband is still by my side and watches over his family, but I am human. I miss his touch, seeing his smile, hearing his voice and the laughter. I miss running into his arms, sharing the passion that we had. I miss going home to him. I miss celebrating all our milestones together. I miss my husband.

I still face struggles every day and I continue to take small steps with one foot in front of the other. For the first three or four months, it was all I could do to put food in my mouth. I had no desire to eat, and hunger pains went away after the first few weeks. I lost too much weight. I would look in the mirror and get discouraged, but what used to bother me now makes me smile and inspires me. I have many stretch marks from childbirth and I had complained about them often. What I see on my body has taken on a whole new meaning. Those are now every day, beautiful reminders of what I was blessed with in this life, and I love them. Our love created those marks. I have the tattoos that also bring me joy. I was Jerry's canvas, and that was the beginning of our artful journey.

Jerry has helped me walk this dark lonely road. He has shared wonderful memories with me that make me laugh. I knew our connection and bond could never be broken. Our love transcends space, time, and dimensions. I still fight battles every day and come out on top. No day is all bad, and no day is all good. I get through each and every one with my faith, hope, and love. This is a journey I would have never chosen to take in my life, but we don't always get to choose.

I still talk to my husband every day. I ask him for help, guidance, and just tell him what I am feeling. There are many moments where I cry and scream. I

A Soulmates Twin Flame

know he is here, and I use my new found spiritual light to help me, but I sometimes feel as if it's not enough. I miss his physical presence, I want the human connection back. I remind myself to look at the gifts I was given, and our new relationship, and I get back up and take another step. I have been shown over and over that there is life after death and Jerry is getting everything ready for when I go home.

Sharing our life and love has brought me great pain and great joy. When I write, I get pulled back into so many happy memories. At times it feels like they happened yesterday. When I finish for the day, I feel an overwhelming pain, knowing that I will never create any new moments with Jerry.

I was shown my purpose in life: to help others and share my journey in hopes that Jerry and I will be an inspiration to all that true fairytale love is real. We created a magic that was beautiful, and through of all this, I was shown the magic that exists outside of what we see and know in life. Jerry and I knew all along that we had something special. We would look at each other, and at the same time we'd both say, "Wow, this is crazy."

I had another dream visit from Jerry that was wonderful. I was in an unknown house looking for him. I didn't know where I was but had a feeling he was there. We had somehow been separated and were looking for each other. I walked around a corner, and there he was sitting on the couch. I stopped walking because I felt like I was not supposed to be there, or he didn't want me there.

I said, "You're here!"

He then looked at me and said, "It's about time, I have been trying to call you."

I walked over to him, he grabbed me and pulled me onto his lap with his arms around me. He kissed me, and then I woke up. It was two o'clock in the morning when I awoke. The dream felt so real and I had butterflies in my

Sarah J Provost

stomach just like he gave me when he was here. I smiled and cried at the same time. I asked him to please come and visit me again, and I tried to go back to sleep.

Through the years I have fallen in love with my husband over and over, and that continues through our spiritual relationship. I am learning and practicing many new things that I have discovered to make our connection even stronger and to communicate with him in the spirit world. I will always love Jerry. We did not separate by choice, and I must follow my feelings that constantly remind me to not give up on life, on love, and our connection. There will come a day when family and friends will celebrate the reunion of Sarah and Jerry.

Until we meet again my love…

I may not see your face or hear your voice but I feel your love surrounding me every day. You will always have my heart and my soul. Jerry, our love has a beginning, but there will never be an end. As I said in our wedding vows, "All the days of my life."

www.ingramcontent.com/pod-product-compliance
Lightning Source LLC
Chambersburg PA
CBHW031412290426
44110CB00011B/353